I0797804

THE FRENCH BASTARDS

THE FRENCH BASTARDS

MODERN PÂTISSERIE CLASSICS FROM PARIS'S CULT BAKERY

Quadrille

FRENCH
Bastards

FOREWORD

THE FRENCH BASTARDS: THE NAME SPEAKS FOR ITSELF!

These guys are crazy, but they're serious about what they do, have lots of good ideas and are ready to shake things up. That's what I said to myself when I first met them a few years ago.

A few weeks after the Oberkampf shop opened, I remember seeing articles in the press about it, and stories and posts all over social media, but I still hadn't met the founders: Julien, David and Manu, the three musketeers of baking!

I was head pastry chef at Fauchon at the time, so I took a few members of my team to meet them early one morning, without warning, just for the pleasure of discovering, savouring and sharing a moment with the new kids from the eleventh arrondissement. I was at once welcomed by Julien, the executive chef and quite a character. After only a few minutes, we were standing in the kitchen with the team, putting the world to rights, when Manu joined us and an immediate friendship was born.

These lovers of bread, of all things pastry and good food in general offer abundance without the fuss. That's what I appreciated right away; in my opinion, it's what you look for most in well-designed bakeries. There's quality, of course, as well as innovation, but above all a generous offering of indulgent sweet treats.

By making their world of ingenuity and skill accessible, this trio has brought a breath of fresh air to the way we present and communicate the world of baking and pastry-making – theirs is a festive and uninhibited version of our profession.

This book is a simple way to discover the magic in their crazy ideas.

LEARN – OBSERVE – LIKE – TRY – START OVER – SAVOUR AND APPRECIATE!

Happy reading,
François Daubinet

CONTENTS

INTRO DUCTION

BEGINNINGS

The French Bastards is essentially the story of three friends with a willingness to flout convention. It all began with Julien Abourmad, a baker and confectioner by training and vocation, with a second CAP (diploma) in chocolate and confectionery. After learning the ropes at La Manufacture de Alain Ducasse chocolate factory and with the luxury caterers Potel & Chabot, he cooked his way around the world with stints in Tel Aviv, Melbourne and Sydney. Julien was amicably given the nickname of 'French Bastard' by the chef Mike McEnearney for his ability to succeed very quickly at anything he set his mind to: whenever the chef set him a task, even if it was something new, he seemed to do it brilliantly and in no time at all. Mike McEnearney is one of Australia's most renowned chefs, owner of the Sydney establishments No. 1 Bent St Sydney and Kitchen by Mike. Julien was working in his bakery at the time, and being called the French Bastard was something of a premonition, the Australian chef unwittingly naming the bakery that was to open in Paris years later. As the nickname was earned some time before the opening, it was Julien's father who recalled it and suggested it to the three partners as the name for their bakery. Appropriately, Australia was where Julien imagined the beginnings of The French Bastards, finding in both its food and uninhibited Anglo-Saxon mindset an endless source of inspiration. The name perfectly expressed their commitment to French baking techniques but carried with it a hint of the irreverence and casualness that characterises them so well. He immediately got in touch with his friend David Abehsera, who without hesitation studied for a CAP in baking after business school. David is a genuine gourmet with a passion not only for finding quality food products but also has a keen interest in French and international food concepts. For a while they toyed with the idea of starting a bakery franchise in Los Angeles, but finally they decided to focus on their own identity in Paris, their hometown. The third member of the trio, art lover Emmanuel Gunther, shaped the brand DNA of The French Bastards while travelling the world during a gap year taken from his studies at the HEC Paris business school. His passions outside the food world bring a creativity and experience that is as innovative as it is multicultural. Together, the trio of Julien, David and Emmanuel are able to defy conventions and build on their differences, combining perfectly to breathe new life into baking.

THE BASTARD SPIRIT

They have set themselves the challenge of reworking the entire Parisian bakery experience: product offering, service, decor, music, packaging… Their aim being to give a new lease of life to the sector by infusing it with inspiration from abroad while staying true to French artisan traditions. Their love of food and travel is obvious and finds expression in each of their creations, which must be bold, tasteful and a feast for the eyes. The French Bastards is a celebration of contrasts and irregularities; nothing is commonplace, which means it is never boring. Keen to hybridise the concept of the bakery, they borrow from other worlds and industries, including restaurants, naturally, and fashion, hotels and nightclubs. Theirs is a perpetual quest for innovation

and a commitment to reinvention every day, which is why they often add the subtitle *Maison Fondée Hier* ('Establishment Founded Yesterday'). The Bastard Spirit pervades all areas of the brand: products, art direction, customer experience, shop design, communications and social media. The French Bastards bring new energy to food porn with images that are both raw and lavish – totally in keeping with their identity – but above all, they have an outspokenness that reflects who they are. Sincerity and authenticity come first. Emmanuel writes every caption for the Instagram posts and responds to every message on social media so it stays true to the brand DNA, down to the smallest detail. Instagram provided a great launch pad in their early days as customers immortalised their experiences in front of the neon sign of The French Bastards. Julien, David and Emmanuel are very attached to their community and are grateful to see that sharing their products on social media allows them to reach an audience well beyond their traditional catchment area. The three co-founders are like free electrons in the French bakery scene; they represent a new generation that plays with French baking and pastry-making conventions without ever losing track of the basics. Their 'bastardry' is a particular blend of irreverence and generosity and, like a sweet tooth, it can never be considered a flaw.

A PLACE THAT MAKES A STATEMENT

The first The French Bastards shop opened in January 2019 on Rue Oberkampf, in Paris's eleventh arrondissement, a district that is very close to their hearts. Improvising as architects, Julien, David and Emmanuel ripped out everything and rebuilt only the essentials. The walls are rough, with the raw materials giving life to the space, and the finishes are almost an afterthought: an identity that perfectly matches their products. On the eve of the opening, they picked objects from the shelves in their own homes as decoration. It's joyous chaos with the feel of a cabinet of curiosities, with Berghain-inspired vinyl records set next to Dragon Ball Z figurines and books of all kinds (from Burning Man to Eckhart Tolle). They've created a place that is very much their own, which draws on their dynamic and impassioned DNA and pop culture and mixes it with international influences. The irreverent trio have hit the right note, and the results are convincing: all their creations sell like hotcakes. Behind the big counter, David and Emmanuel have been welcoming customers for months in this extraordinary, welcoming and convivial atmosphere. Everything is made on site, and the proof can be seen both inside the shop and from the street; you can watch the show in full swing in their gleaming glass kitchen. With AC/DC playing over the speakers, the busy chefs have smiles on their faces and their energy is contagious.

PHILOSOPHY OF THE PRODUCT

The three Bastards may have a very modern vision of baking, but their approach to making bread is old school. After being disappointed by many bakeries, they went back to basics, using natural sourdough and organic flours sustainably produced following traditional methods to create their rustic breads. David is tasked with hand-picking suppliers and meticulously selects the best raw materials to enhance each of Julien's creations. These include stoneground flour, maize flour, white quinoa, black bean flour, hazelnut flour, sometimes a hint of charcoal; there isn't a white baguette in sight. On the contrary, their breads are more indulgent than anything out there: delicious focaccia, thick bâtards and pain de campagne made with hazelnuts, candied orange peel, cranberries and pecans. And above all, no shortcuts are taken; the dough is allowed to rise slowly – for around 48 hours – and is baked thoroughly for a perfect consistency that does justice to the ingredients. When it comes to cakes and pastries, they radiate joy in the form of babkas, moist loaf cakes, cruffins and cinnamon rolls, to name a few. Here you will find opulence and unabashed indulgence. Not to be overlooked are the St-Ho, France's most delectable praline-filled pastry and a spin on the traditional Saint-Honoré, and the BCBG, a lush brioche filled with chocolate-hazelnut spread and cookie dough crumble. The less adventurous can take pleasure in an Isigny butter croissant (semi-inverted laminated dough given six simple turns – just right), as well as a pain au chocolat containing two sticks of Valrhona chocolate or a Granny Smith and New Guinea vanilla apple turnover, among many others. All are devilishly divine creations that showcase quality ingredients, but don't even think about strawberry tarts in winter! The French Bastards' cakes and pastries evolve throughout the year in tune with the seasons and the best produce each of them brings. When it comes to sandwiches, everything revolves around high-quality bread and the best possible fillings. Homemade Brillat-Savarin cream cheese, pickled red onion, speck and rocket go into the focaccia. Label Rouge-certified, traditionally reared chicken is combined with homemade guacamole, 24-month-aged Parmesan and baby spinach in the ciabatta. The unique Prince de Paris ham by Doumbéa joins French Emmental and red coleslaw in the baguette. Only the best will do. Out of a desire for both transparency and to highlight the work of small-scale producers, the exact provenance of the ingredients used in salads and sandwiches is listed on a large blackboard every morning. During their R&D sessions, Julien, David and Emmanuel are always thinking about what looks and feels right. From the very beginning, the customer experience has been of paramount importance, in particular what a product looks like when cut in half. From the way the filling flows out or crumbs are scattered to the cracking sound made by the crust, everything has been designed to transform the enjoyment of a pastry into a truly indulgent experience. This obsession with indulgence has its roots in their Mediterranean origins, a place that celebrates joyous meals, where the abundance of food and sharing brings pleasure. They have all inherited this love of food from their mothers and grandmothers, and from meals where generations come together to eat for hours at a time, leading to full stomachs and smiles on faces. Julien, David and Emmanuel have a common love of rituals where food brings people of all ages together, where the table is covered with plates and old recipes are constantly being revisited and shared. Generous portions, enjoyment of life and deliciousness throughout are the core messages that are conveyed every day in the bakeries.

NEVER GOING ROUND IN CIRCLES

Can the Bastards be called hyperactive? They have six shops that are never empty, collaborations with big names in pastry-making and luxury goods, and they are about to launch of a range of products to take their vision of uninhibited food porn all over France. Collaborations have been an essential part of The French Bastards' identity since the early days. They force the trio of troublemakers to constantly leave their comfort zone to think up even more ways of flouting convention. And by teaming up with partners of choice, they innovate and reach new audiences. Nina Métayer, Nicolas Lambert and François Daubinet have worked closely with Julien and the team at The French Bastards for three consecutive years to create a galette des rois. Through pop-ups and product drops of limited-edition creations, they keep crowds moving all year round. Whether in Rue Oberkampf, Rue Saint-Denis or Place Saint-Ferdinand, they have become both a destination bakery and a neighbourhood landmark.

In short, The French Bastards stand for a generous dose of indulgence, boundless creativity and impeccable sourcing. Three passionate friends with three core values and three Paris shops: The French Bastards still have a lot of surprises in store for us.

Text by Victoire Loup

A NOTE ON GRAMS, SCALES AND USING THESE RECIPES

All of the recipes have been written using grams, as this is far and away the most accurate method for baking, as any pastry chef or keen baker will tell you. Hopefully, you will already own digital scales, but if not, they can be purchased cheaply from any shop (store) or online, and all digital scales have gram measurements, with ounces as an alternative option. You can of course convert to ounces, but given the precision of the measurements, grams will yield the best results. Finally, a note on yeast – all recipes have been written using fresh yeast, but do feel free to convert this to fast-action (dried active) yeast through an online converter.

CHOCOLAT VALRHONA
THÉ GLACÉ BIO JOMO 3.20€
(PECHE-HIBISCUS & CITRON MENTHE GINGEMBRE)
→ LAIT AVOINE + 0,50€
OAT MILK

Nous respectons scrupule
pas de fraisier en hiver, pas de mont-
Notre carte c
parfois au détrime
mais ce n'est q
avant que tu ne jettes to
C'est tout le principe d'une maison
Belleville
Belleville
FORMULES
SANDWICH + BOISSO
SANDWICH + BOISSO
SALADE + BOISSON
SALADE + BOISSON +
PRIX

01

BREA

PASTR

KFAST

IES

CHOCOLATE-HAZELNUT **DOUGHNUTS**

MAKES **6** ✦ PREPARATION TIME: **40 MINS** ✦ COOKING TIME: **10–15 MINS + 5 MINS** ✦ RESTING TIME: **5 HRS 30 MINS**

EQUIPMENT
- **Stand mixer, dough hook**
- **Blender**
- **Baking tray (pan)**
- **Digital food thermometer**
- **Deep fryer (ideally)**
- **Piping bag, plain nozzle**

FOR 1 DOUGHNUT
- **80 g doughnut dough**
- **30 g chocolate-hazelnut spread**

FOR THE DOUGHNUT DOUGH
- **27 g beer**
- **79 g whipping cream (30% fat)**
- **79 g eggs**
- **238 g plain (all-purpose) flour**
- **40 g caster (superfine) sugar**
- **5 g soft light brown sugar**
- **3 g salt**
- **11 g fresh yeast**
- **Oil, for deep frying**
- **Caster (superfine) sugar, to decorate**

FOR THE HAZELNUT PRALINE
- **24 g hazelnuts**
- **22 g caster (superfine) sugar**
- **7 g water**

FOR THE CHOCOLATE-HAZELNUT SPREAD
- **29 g hazelnuts**
- **42 g dark gianduja**
- **42 g milk gianduja**
- **39 g hazelnut praline**
- **6 g unsalted butter**
- **12 g powdered milk**
- **6 g cocoa powder**

1. Make the doughnuts. In a mixer fitted with a dough hook, add the beer, cream and eggs, then add the flour, both sugars, salt and yeast. Run the mixer to form a dough and knead. When the dough comes away from the sides of the bowl, stop the mixer and check the temperature, which should be 23–24°C (73–77°F). Once this temperature is reached, transfer the dough to a container and refrigerate for 3 hours.

2. Divide the dough into 6 pieces each weighing about 80 g (2¾ oz). Place them on a baking tray (pan) and rest in the refrigerator for 30 minutes.

3. Allow to stand at room temperature for 2 hours.

4. Heat the frying oil to 160°C (320°F) in a deep fryer or large pan. Fry the doughnuts for 5–8 minutes on each side.

5. When golden brown, transfer them to paper towel to drain, then roll them in the sugar.

6. To make the praline, roast the hazelnuts for a few minutes in the oven at 180°C (350°F). Allow to cool. Make a light caramel by heating the caster sugar and water. Blend the roasted hazelnuts with the caramel to a runny liquid.

7. To make the chocolate-hazelnut spread, heat a dry frying pan and roast the hazelnuts for a few minutes. Allow to cool. Blend the hazelnuts to a paste.

8. Melt the dark and milk gianduja in a saucepan. Add the hazelnut paste and praline. Mix well. Melt the butter, add it to the mixture, then stir in the milk and cocoa powder. Mix until smooth.

9. Fill each doughnut with 30 g of spread and serve.

Tip
If the praline is not runny enough, you can add a little neutral oil to loosen it.

VANILLA-HAZELNUT PRALINE **DOUGHNUTS**

MAKES **6** ✦ PREPARATION TIME: **40 MINS** ✦ COOKING TIME: **10–15 MINS + 5 MINS** ✦ RESTING TIME: **5 HRS 30 MINS**

EQUIPMENT
- **Stand mixer, dough hook**
- **Blender**
- **Digital food thermometer**
- **Deep fryer (ideally)**
- **Piping bag, plain nozzle**

FOR 1 DOUGHNUT
- **80g dough**
- **30g pastry cream**
- **25g praline**

FOR THE DOUGHNUT DOUGH
- **27g beer**
- **79g whipping cream (30% fat)**
- **79g eggs**
- **238g plain (all-purpose) flour**
- **40g caster (superfine) sugar**
- **5g soft light brown sugar**
- **3g salt**
- **11g fresh yeast**
- **Oil, for deep frying**
- **Caster (superfine) sugar, to decorate**

FOR THE PASTRY CREAM
- **122g whole milk**
- **10g custard powder**
- **24g caster (superfine) sugar**
- **24g egg yolks**
- **1 vanilla pod**

FOR THE PRALINE
- **68g hazelnuts**
- **46g caster (superfine) sugar**
- **16g water**
- **20g whole milk**

1. Make the doughnuts. In a mixer fitted with a dough hook, add the beer, cream and eggs, then add the flour, both sugars, salt and yeast. Run the mixer to form a dough and knead. When the dough comes away from the bowl, stop the mixer and check the temperature, which should be 23–24°C (73–77°F). Once this temperature is reached, transfer the dough to a container and refrigerate for 3 hours.

2. Divide the dough into 6 pieces weighing about 80 g each. Place them on a baking tray (pan) and rest in the refrigerator for 30 minutes.

3. Allow to stand at room temperature for 2 hours.

4. Heat the frying oil to 160°C (320°F) in a deep fryer or large pan. Fry the doughnuts for 5–8 minutes on each side.

5. When golden brown, transfer them to kitchen paper to drain and then roll them in the sugar.

6. To make the pastry cream, bring the milk to a boil in a saucepan. Mix the custard powder and sugar in a bowl. Add the egg yolks to the dry ingredients and whisk until thick and pale. Add half the milk. Whisk to combine, then transfer the mixture to the saucepan with the remaining milk and seeds scraped from the vanilla pod. Bring to the boil, then allow to boil for 35 seconds, stirring constantly to keep the cream from burning. Allow to cool before setting aside in the refrigerator.

7. To make the praline, roast the hazelnuts for a few minutes in the oven at 180°C (350°F). Allow to cool. Make a light caramel by heating the sugar and water. Blend the roasted hazelnuts with the caramel to a runny liquid. Finally, incorporate the milk into the praline.

8. Fill each doughnut with 30 g of pastry cream and 25 g of praline and serve.

Tip

If the praline is not runny enough, you can add a little neutral oil to loosen it.

CHOCOLATE **BABKAS**

MAKES **6** ✦ PREPARATION TIME: **1 HR** ✦ COOKING TIME: **15–18 MINS** ✦ RESTING TIME: **24 HRS + 2 HRS**

EQUIPMENT
- **6 babka moulds**
- **Stand mixer, dough hook**
- **Rolling pin**
- **Pastry brush**

FOR THE BRIOCHE DOUGH
- **250g pastry (sponge) flour**
- **150g eggs**
- **5g salt**
- **53g caster (superfine) sugar**
- **10g whole milk**
- **8g fresh yeast**
- **125g unsalted butter, at room temperature**

FOR THE CHOCOLATE SPREAD
- **8g caster (superfine) sugar**
- **27g unsalted butter**
- **68g dark chocolate couverture (66% cocoa)**
- **8g cocoa powder**

FOR THE SYRUP
- **50g caster (superfine) sugar**
- **50g water**

1. The day before, make the dough. In a mixer fitted with a dough hook, add the flour, eggs, salt, sugar, milk and yeast. Run the mixer to form a dough and knead. When the dough comes away from the sides of the bowl, add the butter and continue to knead. When it comes away again, transfer it to a container and refrigerate overnight.

2. On the day, put all the ingredients for the chocolate spread into a bowl, heat over a bain-marie and stir until smooth.

3. To make the syrup, put the sugar and water into a saucepan and bring to the boil. Transfer the syrup to a container and refrigerate until ready to use.

4. Take the dough out of the refrigerator 20–30 minutes before use. Roll out the dough to a thickness of 3 mm (⅛ in). Cover the entire surface with the chocolate spread, then roll up the dough into a sausage and cut it in half lengthways. Twist the two pieces together, then cut into six pieces (you can use the photos on the next pages as a guide). Place in the moulds and allow to rise for 2 hours.

5. Preheat the oven to 160°C (325°F), then bake for 15–18 minutes.

6. Remove the babkas from the oven, turn them out and brush with cold syrup while still warm.

THE FRENCH
BASTARDS

FRENCH
BASTARDS

BABKAUÈTE
CHOCOLATE & PEANUT BABKAS

MAKES **6** ✦ PREPARATION TIME: **1 HR** ✦ COOKING TIME: **15–18 MINS** ✦ RESTING TIME: **24 HRS + 2 HRS**

EQUIPMENT
- 6 babka moulds
- Stand mixer, dough hook
- Blender
- Rolling pin
- Pastry brush
- Baking parchment

FOR THE BRIOCHE DOUGH
- 250g pastry (sponge) flour
- 150g eggs
- 5g salt
- 53g caster (superfine) sugar
- 10g whole milk
- 8g fresh yeast
- 125g unsalted butter, at room temperature

FOR THE PEANUT PRALINE
- 100g peanuts
- 67g caster (superfine) sugar
- 22g water

FOR THE CHOCOLATE SPREAD
- 8g caster (superfine) sugar
- 27g unsalted butter
- 68g dark chocolate couverture (66% cocoa)
- 8g cocoa powder

FOR THE SYRUP
- 50g caster (superfine) sugar
- 50g water

FOR FINISHING
- 50g whole peanuts

1. The day before, make the dough. In a mixer fitted with a dough hook, add the flour, eggs, salt, sugar, milk and yeast. Run the mixer to form a dough and knead. When the dough comes away from the sides of the bowl, add the butter and continue to knead. When it comes away again, transfer it to a container and refrigerate overnight.

2. On the day, make the praline. Preheat the oven to 180°C (350°F), then roast the peanuts for 10 minutes. Allow to cool. Heat the sugar and water in a saucepan to make a caramel. Add the peanuts and stir until golden brown. Transfer the praline to a sheet of baking parchment and allow to cool. When cold, break it into pieces and blend to a paste.

3. Put all the ingredients for the chocolate spread into a bowl, heat over a bain-marie and stir until smooth.

4. To make the syrup, put the sugar and water into a saucepan and bring to the boil. Transfer the syrup to a container and refrigerate until ready to use.

5. Take the dough out of the refrigerator 20–30 minutes before use. Roll out the dough to a thickness of 3 mm (⅛ in). Cover the entire surface with the chocolate spread, then spread with the praline and scatter over with whole peanuts. Roll up the dough into a sausage and cut it in half lengthways. Twist the two pieces together, then cut into six pieces (you can use the photos on the previous pages as a guide). Place in the moulds and allow to rise for 2 hours.

6. Preheat the oven to 160°C (325°F), then bake for 15–18 minutes.

7. Remove the babkas from the oven, turn out and brush with cold syrup while still warm.

CHOCOLATE CRUMBLE BRIOCHES

MAKES **6** ✦ PREPARATION TIME: **1 HR** ✦ COOKING TIME: **30–40 MINS** ✦ RESTING TIME: **24 HRS + 2 HRS**

EQUIPMENT
- 6 cannelé moulds, 10 cm (4 in) in diameter
- Stand mixer, dough hook, paddle
- Hand-held blender
- Digital food thermometer
- Piping bag, plain nozzle
- Baking tray (pan)
- Pastry brush
- Baking parchment

FOR THE CHOCOLATE BRIOCHE DOUGH
- 326g pastry (sponge) flour
- 33g cocoa powder
- 195g eggs
- 7g salt
- 68g caster (superfine) sugar
- 39g whole milk
- 10g fresh yeast
- 163g unsalted butter, at room temperature

FOR THE CHOCOLATE CRUMBLE
- 35g caster (superfine) sugar
- 35g soft light brown sugar
- 71g unsalted butter
- 71g ground hazelnuts
- 18g cocoa powder

FOR THE VANILLA GANACHE
- 1 vanilla pod
- 209g single (light) cream
- 336g white chocolate
- 54g unsalted butter

1. The day before, make the dough. In a mixer fitted with a dough hook, add the flour, cocoa, eggs, salt, sugar, milk and yeast. Run the mixer to form a dough and knead. When the dough comes away from the sides of the bowl, add the butter and continue to knead. When it comes away again, transfer it to a bowl and refrigerate for 4 hours. Fold the dough to deflate and refrigerate overnight.

2. Now make the vanilla ganache. Split the vanilla pod and scrape out the seeds, then put the pod and seeds into a saucepan with the cream and bring to the boil. Pour the hot liquid over the white chocolate and stir until smooth. When the mixture reaches 40°C (104°F), add the butter, blend and leave to cool. Refrigerate overnight.

3. On the day, divide the dough into six 140-g pieces. Shape into balls and place them on a baking tray (pan) lined with baking parchment. Allow the brioches to rise at room temperature for 2 hours.

4. Preheat the oven to 180°C (350°F). In a mixer fitted with a paddle, mix together all the crumble ingredients to form regular crumbs the size of grains of sand. Transfer the crumble to a baking tray and bake for 15–20 minutes. Set aside at room temperature.

5. Lower the oven temperature to 160°C (325°F). Spread the cooked crumble over the brioches and bake for 20 minutes. Remove from the oven and allow to cool.

6. Transfer the ganache to a piping bag and fill the brioches with a generous amount.

COOKIE-CARAMEL **BRIOCHES**

MAKES **6** ✦ PREPARATION TIME: **2 HRS** ✦ COOKING TIME: **20 MINS** ✦ RESTING TIME: **36 HRS**

EQUIPMENT
- 6 x 3 in pastry rings, 8 cm (3 in) in diameter
- Stand mixer, paddle, dough hook
- Blender
- Piping bag, plain nozzle
- Digital food thermometer
- Pastry brush
- Baking parchment

FOR 1 BRIOCHE
- 80g cookie brioche dough
- 20g cookie dough crumbs
- 40g caramel spread

FOR THE COOKIE DOUGH CRUMBS AND THE SYRUP
- 85g unsalted butter
- 48g vergoise blonde (light caramelised sugar)
- 35g caster (superfine) sugar
- 35g egg
- 99g pastry (sponge) flour
- 7g potato starch
- 4g bicarbonate of soda (baking soda)
- 2g baking powder
- 4 g flaked sea salt
- 123 g milk chocolate couverture (40% cocoa)
- 60g hazelnuts

FOR THE COOKIE BRIOCHE DOUGH
- 129g whole milk
- 36g sunflower oil
- 190g fine soft wheat flour (e.g., Italian 00 flour)
- 30g caster (superfine) sugar
- 2g salt
- 5g fresh yeast
- 88g cookie dough crumbs (see opposite)

FOR THE CARAMEL SPREAD
- 83g whipping cream (30% fat)
- 56g glucose
- 56g caster (superfine) sugar
- 1g salt
- 32g unsalted butter
- 14g cocoa butter

FOR THE GLAZE
- 1 egg, beaten

FOR THE SYRUP
- 50g caster (superfine) sugar
- 50g water

THE FRENCH
BASTARDS
MAISON FONDÉE HIER

MARDI - VENDREDI
8H00 - 20H30
SAMEDI
8H30 - 20H00
DIMANCHE
8H30 - 18H00

COOKIE-CARAMEL **BRIOCHES** (cont.)

1. Two days before, make the cookie dough. In a mixer fitted with a paddle attachment, add the butter, both sugars and eggs, then run the mixer to mix well. In a bowl, mix together the flour, potato starch, bicarbonate of soda, baking powder and salt, then add to the mixer. Mix to combine, then add the chocolate couverture and the hazelnuts. Roll out the dough as thinly as possible on a sheet of baking parchment. Refrigerate overnight.

2. The next day, grind the cookie dough to crumbs in a blender and set aside in the freezer.

3. Now make the brioche dough. In the mixer fitted with the dough hook, combine the milk and oil then add the dry ingredients, except the cookie dough crumbs (add the yeast last). Run the mixer to form a dough and knead. When the dough comes away from the bowl, stop the mixer and check the temperature, which should be 23–24°C (73–77°F). Add the cookie dough crumbs and knead for a further 2 minutes. Transfer the brioche dough to a bowl and refrigerate overnight. Set aside the remaining cookie dough crumbs.

4. Next, make the caramel spread. Heat the cream in a saucepan and set aside. In a second saucepan, cook the glucose, sugar and salt until the mixture turns a rich caramel colour. Add the hot cream. When the mixture reaches 70°C (158°F), stir in the butter and cocoa butter. Blend and refrigerate overnight.

5. On the day, make the brioches. Take the brioche dough out of the refrigerator and divide it into six 80 g pieces. Place each piece in a pastry ring. Allow to rise at room temperature for 3 hours.

6. Preheat the oven to 160°C (325°F). Brush the buns with the beaten egg and scatter cookie dough crumble over the top. Place the brioches on a baking tray (pan) lined with baking parchment and bake for 20 minutes.

7. Meanwhile, make a syrup. Combine the sugar and water in a saucepan and bring to the boil. Transfer the syrup to a container and refrigerate until ready to use.

8. Turn out the brioches while still warm and brush them with the syrup. Allow to cool.

9. When cold, use a piping bag to fill the brioches with plenty of caramel spread.

CHOCOLATE **FONDANTS**

MAKES **6** ✦ PREPARATION TIME: **20 MINS** ✦ COOKING TIME: **10 MINS**

EQUIPMENT
- **6 individual moulds**
- **Hand mixer**
- **Baking tray (pan)**
- **Baking parchment**

FOR THE CHOCOLATE CAKE BATTER
- **181g unsalted butter**
- **259g dark chocolate**
- **128g icing (powdered) sugar**
- **77g plain (all-purpose) flour**
- **259g eggs**
- **60g hazelnuts**
- **60g almonds**

1. Preheat the oven to 160°C (325°F). Place the hazelnuts and almonds on a baking tray (pan) lined with baking parchment and roast for 15 minutes.

2. Meanwhile, melt the butter and chocolate over a bain-marie. Combine the icing sugar and flour in a bowl, add the eggs and beat until smooth. Then add the chocolate mixture and mix to combine.

3. Grease the moulds and use a spoon to fill them with the batter. Scatter with the roasted almonds and hazelnuts. Bake for at least 10 minutes. Adjust the cooking time according to how runny you want the fondants to be.

Tip

After baking, you can add a little praline (see recipes on pages 16 and 17) for a decadence worthy of being called food porn!

BROWKIES

MAKES **6** ✦ PREPARATION TIME: **30 MINS** ✦ COOKING TIME: **15 MINS** ✦ RESTING TIME: **OVERNIGHT**

EQUIPMENT
- **6 individual moulds**
- **Stand mixer, paddle**
- **Baking parchment**

FOR 1 BROWKIE
- **150g browkie batter**
- **88g cookie dough crumbs**

FOR THE COOKIE DOUGH CRUMBS
- **102g unsalted butter**
- **57g vergoise blonde (light caramelised sugar)**
- **42g caster (superfine) sugar**
- **35g egg**
- **118g pastry (sponge) flour**
- **8g potato starch**
- **4g bicarbonate of soda (baking soda)**
- **2g baking powder**
- **4 g flaked sea salt**
- **148g milk chocolate (45% cocoa)**
- **72g hazelnuts**

FOR THE BROWKIE BATTER
- **86g unsalted butter**
- **172g chocolate (64% cocoa)**
- **65g plain (all-purpose) flour**
- **2g baking powder**
- **160g eggs**
- **257g soft light brown sugar**
- **23g cocoa powder**
- **1g salt**
- **137g cookie dough crumbs (see above)**

1. The day before, make the cookie dough. In a mixer fitted with a paddle, add the butter, both sugars and egg and run the mixer to combine without beating. In a bowl, mix together the flour, potato starch, bicarbonate of soda, baking powder and salt, then add to the mixer. Mix to combine, then add the chocolate in pieces and the hazelnuts. Roll out the dough as thinly as possible on a sheet of baking parchment. Freeze overnight.

2. On the day, chop the cookie dough into crumbs and set aside in the freezer. Part of the mixture will be used to make the browkies and the rest will be used as a topping.

3. Make the browkies. Melt the butter and chocolate over a bain-marie. Mix the flour with the baking powder. Whisk the eggs with the sugar until thick and pale, then add the chocolate mixture. Add the cocoa powder, salt, flour and baking powder. Stir in 137 g of frozen cookie dough crumbs. Set aside the remainder.

4. Preheat the oven to 180°C (350°F). Fill the moulds with the browkie batter. Scatter with the remaining cookie cough crumbs and bake for no longer than 15 minutes if you want the centre to remain soft. Allow to cool before serving.

Tip

Don't hesitate to add chocolate-hazelnut spread (see the recipes on pages 17 and 40) to the top for even more indulgence!

CHOCOLATE-HAZELNUT **COOKIES**

MAKES **6** ✦ PREPARATION TIME: **30 MINS** ✦ COOKING TIME: **15 MINS** ✦ RESTING TIME: **ABOUT 1 HR**

EQUIPMENT
- **Stand mixer, paddle attachment**
- **Dome moulds or a baking tray**
- **Blender**
- **Piping bag**
- **Baking parchment**

FOR 1 COOKIE
- **100g cookie dough crumbs**
- **20g chocolate-hazelnut spread**

FOR THE COOKIE DOUGH
- **102g unsalted butter**
- **57g vergoise blonde (light caramelised sugar)**
- **42g caster (superfine) sugar**
- **35g egg**
- **118g pastry (sponge) flour**
- **8g potato starch**
- **4g bicarbonate of soda (baking soda)**
- **2g baking powder**
- **4 g flaked sea salt**
- **148g milk chocolate (38% cocoa)**
- **72g hazelnuts**

FOR THE HAZELNUT PRALINE
- **15g hazelnuts**
- **9g caster (superfine) sugar**
- **4g water**

FOR THE CHOCOLATE-HAZELNUT SPREAD
- **20g hazelnuts**
- **5g unsalted butter**
- **28g dark gianduja**
- **28g milk gianduja**
- **29g hazelnut praline (see above)**
- **8g powdered milk**
- **4g cocoa powder**

1. Roast all the hazelnuts for a few minutes in the oven at 180°C (350°F). Weigh out 15 g for the praline and 20 g for the spread.

2. Make the cookie dough. In a mixer fitted with a paddle attachment, combine the butter, both sugars and the egg.
In a bowl, mix together the flour, potato starch, bicarbonate of soda, baking powder and salt, then add to the mixer. Run the mixer to combine, then add the chocolate in pieces and 37 g of the hazelnuts. Roll out the dough as thinly as possible on a sheet of baking parchment. Refrigerate until ready to use.

3. For the praline, make a light caramel by heating the sugar with the water. Pour it over the 15 g of hazelnuts. Allow the mixture to cool, then blend to a runny liquid.

4. To make the chocolate-hazelnut spread, grind the remaining 20 g of roasted hazelnuts in a blender. Melt the dark and milk gianduja in a saucepan and add the ground hazelnuts. Mix well. Stir in the praline, milk and cocoa. Mix with a spatula until smooth.

5. Fill a piping bag with the spread and pipe about 20 g into each dome mould or mounds of the same weight over a baking tray lined with baking parchment. Place in the freezer for about an hour until the spread is completely frozen.

6. Preheat the oven to 180°C (350°F). Shape six 100 g portions of cookie dough into balls and press the chocolate-hazelnut spread insert into the centre. Place the filled dough balls on a baking tray (pan). Bake for 15 minutes. Allow to cool slightly before serving.

CARAMEL-MACADAMIA **CHOCOLATE COOKIES**

MAKES **6** ✦ PREPARATION TIME: **30 MINS** ✦ COOKING TIME: **15 MINS** ✦ RESTING TIME: **24 HRS + 1 HR**

EQUIPMENT
- **Hand-held blender**
- **Stand mixer, paddle attachment**
- **Piping bag**
- **Baking parchment**

FOR 1 COOKIE
- **100 g chocolate cookie dough**
- **20 g caramel**
- **8 g macadamia nuts**

FOR THE CARAMEL
- **41 g cream (30% fat)**
- **28 g glucose**
- **28 g caster (superfine) sugar**
- **16 g unsalted butter**
- **7 g cocoa butter**

FOR THE COOKIE DOUGH
- **102 g unsalted butter**
- **57 g vergoise blonde (light caramelised sugar)**
- **42 g caster (superfine) sugar**
- **42 g egg**
- **95 g plain (all-purpose) flour**
- **23 g cocoa powder**
- **8 g potato starch**
- **4 g bicarbonate of soda (baking soda)**
- **2 g baking powder**
- **4 g flaked sea salt**
- **148 g milk chocolate couverture (38% cocoa)**
- **72 g macadamia nuts**

FOR FINISHING
- **A handful macadamia nuts, finely chopped**

1. The day before, make the caramel. Heat the cream in a saucepan. In another saucepan, cook the glucose and sugar to a rich caramel. Add the hot cream, then add the butter and blend. Blend in the cocoa butter. Refrigerate for 24 hours.

2. On the day, make the cookie dough. In a mixer fitted with a paddle attachment, combine the butter, both sugars and the egg. In a bowl, mix together the flour, cocoa, potato starch, bicarbonate of soda, baking powder and salt, then add to the mixer. Using a knife, chop the chocolate and nuts into nice chunks and incorporate them into the dough. Rest the dough in the refrigerator for 1 hour.

3. Preheat the oven to 180°C (350°F). Shape six 100 g portions of cookie dough into balls. Place them on a baking tray (pan) lined with baking parchment and bake for 15 minutes. Remove from the oven and allow to cool.

4. Fill a piping bag with the caramel and decorate the cookies. Finely chop the nuts and add them to the cookies.

FRENCH
Bastards
Kevin Nguyen
Pastry Chef

CARAMEL-PRALINE **KUGELHOPFS**

MAKES **6** ✦ PREPARATION TIME: **30 MINS** ✦ COOKING TIME: **15–18 MINS** ✦ RESTING TIME: **1 HR 30 MINS**

EQUIPMENT
- **Blender**
- **6 individual kugelhopf moulds**
- **Stand mixer, dough hook**

FOR THE ALMOND PRALINE
- **37g almonds**
- **25g caster (superfine) sugar**
- **9g water**

FOR THE KUGELHOPF DOUGH
- **236g pastry (sponge) flour**
- **142g eggs**
- **50g caster (superfine) sugar**
- **5g salt**
- **9g whole milk**
- **7g fresh yeast**
- **118g unsalted butter**
- **71g almond praline (see above)**
- **24g Sosa® crispy caramel (freeze-dried caramel crispies)**

1. To make the praline, roast the almonds for a few minutes in the oven at 180°C (350°F). Heat the water and sugar in a saucepan and add the roasted almonds. Stir with a spatula to caramelise the almonds. Transfer them to a bowl and allow to cool before blending to a very coarse praline.

2. Make the kugelhopf dough. In a mixer fitted with a dough hook, mix the flour, eggs, sugar, salt, milk and yeast to form a dough. Knead until the dough comes away from the sides of the bowl, then add the butter. Continue to knead until the dough comes away again, then incorporate the praline and crispy caramel. Transfer the dough to a bowl and rest in the refrigerator for 1 hour 30 minutes.

3. Shape six 110 g portions of dough into balls. Make a hole in the centre of each dough ball and insert the balls into the moulds. Allow the dough to rise at 28°C (82°F). In winter, use your oven after first heating it to this temperature with a container of hot water.

4. Preheat the oven to 160°C (325°F). Bake for 15–18 minutes.

Tip

After turning them out, you can fill the hole in each kugelhopf with caramel (see page 110) before serving.

BUTTER **CROISSANTS**

MAKES **6** ✦ PREPARATION TIME: **1 HR** ✦ COOKING TIME: **20 MINS** ✦ RESTING TIME: **2 HRS 15 MINS**

EQUIPMENT
- **Stand mixer, dough hook**
- **Rolling pin**
- **Baking tray (pan)**
- **Cling film (plastic wrap), baking parchment**

FOR THE CROISSANT DOUGH
- **128g pastry (sponge) flour**
- **128g fine soft wheat flour (e.g., Italian 00 flour)**
- **5g salt**
- **10g fresh yeast**
- **12g unsalted butter, chilled**
- **38g caster (superfine) sugar**
- **7g cold water**
- **105g whole milk, cold**
- **13g whole egg**
- **154g unsalted dry butter (84% fat)**

FOR THE GLAZE
- **1 egg, beaten**

1. In the mixer fitted with the dough hook, combine all the ingredients for the dough, except the dry butter. Run the mixer on the lowest speed for 5 minutes to form a dough, then knead on low-medium speed for 8 minutes. The dough should be smooth.

2. Shape the dough into a rectangle on a baking tray (pan). Wrap in cling film (plastic wrap), allowing the cling film to be in contact with the dough, and rest for 15 minutes in the refrigerator.

3. Take the dough out of the refrigerator and use it to encase the dry butter. Make a double turn by folding the dough into quarters, like a book, then roll it out to a thickness of 8 mm (⅓ in). Next, make a simple turn by folding the dough into thirds, like a letter, and then roll it out to a thickness of 4 mm (⅛ in). Follow the step-by-step instructions and photographs on pages 152–153 as a guide, as the same technique for folding and turning dough is used.

4. Cut out six triangles measuring 9 × 29 × 29 cm (3½ × 11½ × 11½ in). Each should weigh 100 g. Starting at the widest part, roll the triangles into croissants, finishing with the tip.

5. Lay the croissants on a baking tray lined with baking parchment and leave to rise for 2 hours.

6. When they have doubled in size, preheat the oven to 150°C (300°F).

7. Glaze the croissants by brushing with the beaten egg and bake for 20 minutes.

CHOCOLATE CRUFFINS

MAKES **6** ✦ PREPARATION TIME: **1 HR** ✦ COOKING TIME: **25 MINS** ✦ RESTING TIME: **24 HRS + 2 HRS 15 MINS**

EQUIPMENT
- 6 round moulds, 9 cm (3½ in) in diameter and 4 cm (1½ in) deep
- Stand mixer, dough hook
- Hand-held blender
- Baking tray (pan)
- Rolling pin
- Piping bag, plain nozzle
- Cling film (plastic wrap)

FOR 1 CRUFFIN
- 100 g croissant dough
- 35 g milk chocolate ganache
- 1 g cocoa powder

FOR THE MILK CHOCOLATE GANACHE
- 84 g cream (30% fat)
- 7 g inverted sugar
- 5 g glucose
- 97 g milk chocolate (38% cocoa)
- 17 g unsalted butter

FOR THE CROISSANT DOUGH
- 25 g cocoa nibs
- Around 118 g milk
- 131 g strong white flour
- 131 g pastry (sponge) flour
- 6 g salt
- 11 g fresh yeast
- 13 g unsalted butter
- 41 g caster (superfine) sugar
- 8 g water
- 14 g egg
- 17 g cocoa powder
- 84 g Isigny (Normandy) butter

FOR FINISHING
- Cocoa powder

1. The day before, make the ganache. Combine the cream, inverted sugar and glucose in a saucepan and bring to the boil. Add the chocolate, blend, and stir in the butter. Refrigerate for 24 hours before use.

2. Soak the cocoa nibs in the milk for 24 hours. Strain the milk through a sieve and make it up, once again, to 118 g.

3. On the day, make the croissant dough. Sieve the flour into a mixer fitted with a dough hook. Add the milk and combine with all the other ingredients, except the Isigny butter. Mix on the lowest speed for 5 minutes to form a dough, then knead on low-medium speed for 8 minutes. The dough should be smooth.

4. Shape the dough into a rectangle on a baking tray (pan). Cover in cling film (plastic wrap), allowing it to be in direct contact with the dough, and rest for 10–15 minutes in the refrigerator.

5. Take the dough out of the refrigerator and use it to encase the Isigny butter. Make a double turn and roll out the dough to a thickness of 8 mm (⅓ in). Next, make a simple turn and roll it out to a thickness of 8 mm (⅓ in). Then roll out the dough to a 4 mm (⅛ in) thickness with a width of 35 cm (13½ in). At the top and bottom of the dough, across the width, mark out six 4.5 cm wide strips, then cut them out. Follow the step-by-step instructions and photographs on pages 152–153 as a guide, as the same technique for folding and turning dough is used. Arrange in the moulds and allow to rise for 2 hours, until doubled in size.

6. Preheat the oven to 150°C (300°F) and bake for 25 minutes.

7. Transfer the ganache to a piping bag fitted with the nozzle and fill the cruffins. Dust with cocoa powder.

BAKED

LEMON MERINGUE **CRUFFINS**

MAKES **6** ✦ PREPARATION TIME: **1 HR** ✦ COOKING TIME: **20–25 MINS** ✦ RESTING TIME: **24 HRS + 2 HRS 15 MINS**

EQUIPMENT
- 6 round moulds, 9 cm (3½ in) in diameter and 4 cm (1½ in) deep
- Stand mixer, dough hook, whisk
- Hand-held blender
- Digital food thermometer
- Baking tray (pan)
- Rolling pin
- Piping bag, plain nozzle
- Blowtorch
- Cling film (plastic wrap)

FOR 1 CRUFFIN
- 100g croissant dough
- 35g lemon cream
- 36g Italian meringue

FOR THE LEMON CREAM
- 45g caster (superfine) sugar
- 38g egg
- 45g lemon juice
- 81g unsalted butter

FOR THE CROISSANT DOUGH
- 128g pastry (sponge) flour
- 128g fine soft wheat flour (e.g., Italian 00 flour)
- 5g salt
- 10g fresh yeast
- 12g unsalted butter
- 38g caster (superfine) sugar
- 7g cold water
- 106g whole milk, cold
- 13g egg
- 154g unsalted dry butter (84% fat)

FOR THE MERINGUE
- 120g caster (superfine) sugar
- 40g water
- 60g egg whites

1. The day before, make the lemon cream. In a bowl over a bain-marie, mix the sugar, egg and lemon juice until the mixture thickens. The temperature must reach 85°C (185°F) without going any higher. Remove from the heat and incorporate the butter using a hand-held blender. Refrigerate for 24 hours.

2. On the day, make the croissant dough. In a mixer fitted with a dough hook, combine all the ingredients except the dry butter. Mix on the lowest speed for 5 minutes to form a dough, then knead on a low-medium speed for 8 minutes. The dough should be smooth.

3. Shape the dough into a rectangle on a baking tray (pan). Cover with cling film (plastic wrap), allowing it to be in direct contact with the dough and rest for 10–15 minutes in the refrigerator.

4. Take the dough out of the refrigerator and use it to encase the dry butter. Make a double turn and roll out the dough to a thickness of 8 mm (⅓ in). Next, make a simple turn and roll it out to a thickness of 8 mm (⅓ in). Then roll out the dough to a 4 mm (⅛ in) thickness with a width of 35 cm (13½ in). At the top and bottom of the dough, across the width, mark out six 4.5 cm (1¾ in) wide strips, then cut them out. Follow the step-by-step instructions and photographs on pages 152–153 as a guide, as the same technique for folding and turning dough is used. Roll up the strips without pressing to allow the layers to separate.

5. Arrange in the moulds and let rise for 2 hours, until doubled in size.

6. Preheat the oven to 150°C (300°F) and bake for 20–25 minutes.

7. Allow the cruffins to cool. Then, using a piping bag, fill them with lemon cream (from the top).

8. Make the meringue. Heat the water and sugar in a saucepan to 121°C (250°F). In the mixer fitted with the whisk, beat the egg whites until foamy, then add the syrup in a thin stream. Increase the speed to high and beat until the meringue has cooled to lukewarm and has an elastic consistency.

9. Using a spatula, spread meringue over the top of each cruffin. Carefully caramelise the meringue, using a blowtorch.

PAINS AUX RAISINS

MAKES **6** ✦ PREPARATION TIME: **1 HR** ✦ COOKING TIME: **25 MINS** ✦ RESTING TIME: **2 HRS 15 MINS**

EQUIPMENT
- **Stand mixer, dough hook**
- **Rolling pin**
- **Cling film (plastic wrap), baking parchment**

FOR 1 PAIN AUX RAISINS
- **110g croissant dough**
- **170g pastry cream**
- **100g currants**

FOR THE PASTRY CREAM
- **112g whole milk**
- **21g caster (superfine) sugar**
- **10g custard powder**
- **4g egg yolk**
- **22g whole egg**

FOR THE CROISSANT DOUGH
- **141g pastry (sponge) flour**
- **141g fine soft wheat flour (e.g., Italian 00 flour)**
- **6g salt**
- **11g fresh yeast**
- **14g unsalted butter, cold**
- **42g caster (superfine) sugar**
- **7g cold water**
- **116g whole milk, cold**
- **14g egg**
- **169g unsalted dry butter (84% fat)**

FOR FINISHING
- **600g currants**

FOR THE SYRUP
- **150g caster (superfine) sugar**
- **150g water**

1. Make the pastry cream. Pour the milk into a saucepan and bring to the boil. Combine the sugar and custard powder in a bowl, add the egg yolk and whole egg and mix well. Pour in half the hot milk, stir to combine, then return the mixture to the pan with the remaining milk. Bring back to the boil, then remove from the heat. Allow to cool.

2. In a mixer fitted with a dough hook, combine all the ingredients for the dough, except the dry butter. Mix on the lowest speed for 5 minutes to form a dough, then knead on speed 2 for 8 minutes. The dough should be smooth.

3. Shape the dough into a rectangle on a baking tray (pan). Cover with cling film (plastic wrap), allowing it to be in direct contact with the dough and rest for 15 minutes in the refrigerator.

4. Take the dough out of the refrigerator and use it to encase the dry butter. Make a double turn and roll out the dough to a thickness of 8 mm (⅓ in). Next, make a simple turn and roll it out to a thickness of 8 mm (⅓ in), then roll out the dough to a thickness of 4.5 mm (⅓ in). Follow the step-by-step instructions and photographs on pages 152–153 as a guide, as the same technique for folding and turning dough is used. Trim the edges of the dough to form a regular rectangle. Press the lower edge of the dough with your fingers.

5. Using a spatula, spread the pastry cream over the entire surface of the dough. Scatter the currants evenly over the cream. Starting at the top, roll the dough into a sausage, then cut it into six slices. Lay the slices on a baking tray lined with baking parchment and leave to rise for 2 hours.

6. When they have doubled in size, preheat the oven to 150°C (300°F) and bake for 25 minutes.

7. In the meantime, make the syrup. Combine the sugar and water in a saucepan and heat until the sugar dissolves. Allow to cool. Remove the pains aux raisins from the oven and brush them while still hot with the cold syrup.

THE FRENCH BASTARDS
CINNAMON ROLLS

MAKES **6** ✦ PREPARATION TIME: **30 MINS** ✦ COOKING TIME: **15–18 MINS** ✦ RESTING TIME: **OVERNIGHT + 2 HRS**

EQUIPMENT
- **6 brioche moulds**
- **Stand mixer, dough hook, whisk**
- **Rolling pin**

FOR 1 CINNAMON ROLL
- **500g brioche dough**
- **140g cinnamon filling**
- **150g icing**

FOR THE BRIOCHE DOUGH
- **125g eggs**
- **8g whole milk**
- **6g fresh yeast**
- **208g pastry (sponge) flour**
- **44g caster (superfine) sugar**
- **4g salt**
- **104g unsalted butter**

FOR THE CINNAMON FILLING
- **45g unsalted butter**
- **11g plain (all-purpose) flour**
- **34g egg**
- **45g caster (superfine) sugar**
- **5g ground cinnamon**

FOR THE ICING
- **120g icing (powdered) sugar**
- **30 ml water**

1. The day before, make the dough. In a mixer fitted with a dough hook, combine the eggs, milk, yeast, flour, sugar and salt. Mix on the lowest speed for 5 minutes to form a dough, then knead on low-medium speed for 7 minutes. Gradually add the butter in small pieces and knead until well incorporated. When the dough comes away from the sides of the bowl, transfer it to a container and refrigerate overnight.

2. On the day, make the cinnamon filling. Melt the butter and set it aside to cool slightly. In the mixer fitted with the whisk, add the flour, egg, sugar and cinnamon. Beat until the mixture is foamy. With the mixer running, gradually add the melted butter, beating until smooth. Transfer the filling to a container and refrigerate until ready to use.

3. Take the dough out of the refrigerator, roll out to a thickness of 3 mm (⅛ in) and rest in the refrigerator for 30 minutes.

4. Spread the cinnamon filling over the entire surface of the dough, roll up into a sausage and cut into six slices. Arrange in the moulds and allow to rise for 1 hour 30 minutes, until doubled in size.

5. Preheat the oven to 150°C (300°F) and bake for 15–18 minutes.

6. Meanwhile, make the icing by mixing the icing sugar and water. Remove the rolls from the oven, brush with the icing and return to the oven for 1 minute at 90°C (200°F).

02

DESS

ERTS

FIG & PISTACHIO TARTE BOULANGÈRE

SERVES **6** ✦ PREPARATION TIME: **2 HRS** ✦ COOKING TIME: **15–20 MINS** ✦ RESTING TIME: **24 HRS + 5 HRS**

EQUIPMENT
- **Stand mixer, dough hook, paddle**
- **Baking tray (pan)**
- **1 square baking tin (pan)**
- **Piping bag**
- **Rolling pin**
- **Cling film (plastic wrap), baking parchment**

FOR 1 TART
- **331g puff pastry**
- **150g pistachio and almond cream**
- **360g figs**
- **24g pistachio nuts**
- **5g glaze**

FOR THE PUFF PASTRY
- **47g water**
- **3g white vinegar**
- **3g salt**
- **2g caster (superfine) sugar**
- **92g plain (all-purpose) flour**
- **46g pastry (sponge) flour**
- **138g unsalted dry butter (84% fat)**

FOR THE PISTACHIO-ALMOND CREAM
- **45g unsalted butter, at room temperature**
- **45g caster (superfine) sugar**
- **22g ground almonds (almond flour)**
- **22g ground pistachios**
- **45g egg**

FOR THE GLAZE
- **400g apricot glaze**
- **40g water**

TO FINISH
- **360g figs**
- **24g pistachio nuts, finely chopped**

1. Leave the dry butter at room temperature for 12 hours before use.

2. Make the détrempe and beurre manié the day before you plan to make the puff pastry. To make the détrempe, combine the water, vinegar, salt, sugar and plain flour in a mixer fitted with a dough hook. Mix and knead to a smooth dough. Roll out the dough into a square and place on a baking tray (pan) lined with baking parchment. Cover with cling film (plastic wrap), allowing it to be in direct contact with the dough and refrigerate overnight.

3. In the mixer fitted with the paddle, combine the softened dry butter with the pastry flour and mix to a smooth paste that is easy to handle. Roll out the beurre manié to an even thickness. Refrigerate overnight.

4. On the day, roll out the détrempe to a width and length that will allow the beurre manié to be fully covered. Place the butter in the middle of the dough and fold the sides over to encase the butter. Make three simple turns (follow the step-by-step instructions and photographs on pages 152–153 as a guide). Refrigerate for at least 5 hours.

5. Make another three simple turns, then roll out the pastry to a thickness of 3 mm (⅛ in).

6. Make the pistachio-almond cream. Mix the softened butter with the sugar, ground almonds and pistachios until smooth, then incorporate the egg.

7. Prepare the glaze by heating the apricot glaze with the water in a small saucepan. Mix and set aside.

8. Preheat the oven to 180°C (350°F). Grease the square baking tin (pan) with butter and line it with the puff pastry. Spread the pistachio and almond cream over the entire surface and arrange the figs on top. Bake for 15–20 minutes, until the puff pastry turns golden brown.

9. Drizzle the glaze over the fruit and scatter with the pistachios.

HAZELNUT **SWEET PASTRY**

MAKES **1 TART CASE TO SERVE 6 OR 6 TARTLET CASES** ✦ PREPARATION TIME: **20 MINS**
COOKING TIME: **18–20 MINS** ✦ RESTING TIME: **4 HRS**

EQUIPMENT
- **1 tart tin (pan) or 6 tart rings**
- **Cling film (plastic wrap)**

FOR THE PASTRY
- **143 g plain (all-purpose) flour**
- **34 g icing (powdered) sugar**
- **22 g caster (superfine) sugar**
- **22 g ground hazelnuts**
- **79 g unsalted butter**
- **31 g egg**

1. Mix together the flour, icing sugar, sugar, ground hazelnuts and butter to very fine crumbs. Incorporate the egg.

2. Shape the dough into a ball, wrap in cling film (plastic wrap) and refrigerate for at least 4 hours.

3. Roll out the dough to a thickness of 3 mm (⅛ in).

4. Preheat the oven to 160°C (325°F). Cut the dough to the size of the tart mould(s) you will be using.

5. Grease the mould(s) before lining with the dough.

6. Bake in the oven for 18–20 minutes.

STRAWBERRY-LEMON **TARTLETS**

MAKES **6** ✦ PREPARATION TIME: **1 HR** ✦ COOKING TIME: **18–20 MINS** ✦ RESTING TIME: **OVERNIGHT + 4 HRS**

EQUIPMENT
- **6 tart rings, 8 cm (3 in) in diameter and 3 cm (1¼ in) deep**
- **Hand-held blender**
- **Rolling pin**
- **Digital food thermometer**
- **Cling film (plastic wrap)**

FOR 1 TARTLET
- **55g hazelnut sweet pastry**
- **40g lemon cream**
- **25g strawberry jam**
- **50g fresh strawberries**
- **2g Vene Cress**

FOR THE HAZELNUT SWEET PASTRY
- **143g plain (all-purpose) flour**
- **34g icing (powdered) sugar**
- **22g caster (superfine) sugar**
- **22g ground hazelnuts**
- **79g unsalted butter**
- **31g egg**

FOR THE LEMON CREAM
- **52g lemon juice**
- **52g caster (superfine) sugar**
- **43g egg**
- **93g unsalted butter**

FOR THE STRAWBERRY JAM
- **108g strawberry purée**
- **18g caster (superfine) sugar**
- **2g pectin NH**
- **22g lemon juice**

TO FINISH
- **300g fresh strawberries**
- **12g Vene Cress**

1. The day before, make the sweet pastry. Mix together the flour, icing sugar, caster sugar, ground hazelnuts and butter to very fine crumbs. Incorporate the egg. Shape the dough into a ball, wrap in cling film and refrigerate for at least 4 hours.

2. Preheat the oven to 160°C (325°F). Roll out the dough to a thickness of 3 mm (⅛ in). Cut out six 12 cm diameter discs. Grease the tart rings, then line them with the dough. Bake the tartlet cases for 18–20 minutes, then allow to cool.

3. Meanwhile, make the lemon cream. Heat the lemon juice with the sugar and egg in a heatproof bowl set over a pan of simmering water. Blend the butter into the hot mixture.

4. Add 40 g lemon cream to each tartlet case. Refrigerate overnight to allow the cream to set.

5. On the day, make the strawberry jam. In a saucepan, heat the strawberry purée and lemon juice to 45°C (113°F). Mix the sugar with the pectin, add to the saucepan and bring to the boil.

6. Fill the tartlet cases with the jam. Cut up the strawberries and arrange them randomly on top of each tartlet, then garnish with the cress.

LEMON MERINGUE **TARTLETS**

MAKES **6** ✦ PREPARATION TIME: **1 HR** ✦ COOKING TIME: **18–20 MINS** ✦ RESTING TIME: **OVERNIGHT + 4 HRS**

EQUIPMENT

- **6 tart rings, 8 cm (3 in) in diameter and 3 cm (1¼ in) deep**
- **Stand mixer, whisk**
- **Hand-held blender**
- **Blowtorch**
- **Rolling pin**
- **Digital food thermometer**
- **Cling film (plastic wrap)**

FOR 1 TARTLET

- **55g hazelnut sweet pastry**
- **40g lemon cream**
- **25g Italian meringue**

FOR THE HAZELNUT SWEET PASTRY

- **143g plain (all-purpose) flour**
- **34g icing (powdered) sugar**
- **22g caster (superfine) sugar**
- **22g ground hazelnuts**
- **79g unsalted butter**
- **31g egg**

FOR THE LEMON CREAM

- **52g lemon juice**
- **52g caster (superfine) sugar**
- **43g egg**
- **93g unsalted butter**

FOR THE MERINGUE

- **48g egg whites**
- **19g water**
- **82g caster (superfine) sugar**

1. The day before, make the sweet pastry. Mix together the flour, icing sugar, caster sugar, ground hazelnuts and butter to very fine crumbs. Incorporate the egg. Shape the dough into a ball, wrap in cling film and refrigerate for 4 hours.

2. Preheat the oven to 160°C (325°F). Roll out the dough to a thickness of 3 mm (⅛ in). Cut out six 12 cm (4½ in) diameter discs. Grease the tart rings, then line them with the dough. Bake the tartlet cases for 18–20 minutes, then allow to cool.

3. Meanwhile, make the lemon cream. Combine the lemon juice, sugar and egg in a heatproof bowl set over a pan of simmering water and heat to 85°C (185°F). Blend the butter into the hot mixture. Fill the tartlet cases with the cream. Refrigerate overnight to allow the cream to set.

4. On the day, make the meringue. Put the egg whites into the bowl of a mixer fitted with a whisk. Heat the water and sugar in a saucepan. When the temperature reaches 110°C (230°F), start beating the egg whites to soft peaks on the lowest speed. When the syrup reaches 121°C (250°F), add in a thin stream to the beaten egg whites.

5. When all the syrup has been incorporated, run the mixer on the highest speed. When the consistency of the meringue seems ideal – a little elastic – allow it cool a little, then add it to the top of the tartlets. Using the blowtorch, caramelise the meringue, taking care not to burn yourself.

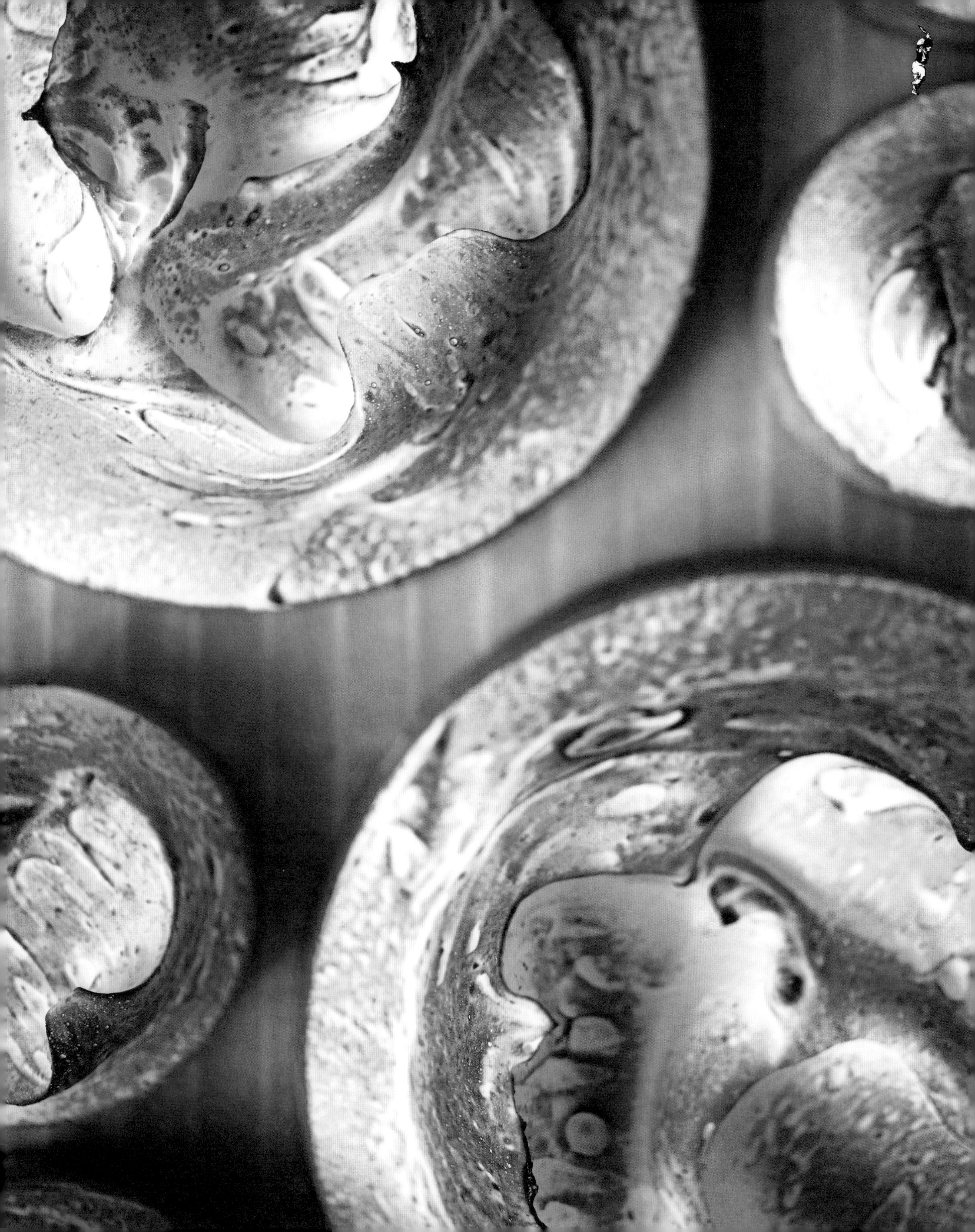

VANILLA SAINT-HONORÉS

MAKES **6** ✦ PREPARATION TIME: **2 HRS** ✦ COOKING TIME: **30–32 MINS** ✦ RESTING TIME: **24 HRS + 4 HRS**

EQUIPMENT
- 6 tart rings, 8 cm (3 in) in diameter and 3 cm (1¼ in) deep
- Stand mixer, whisk, paddle
- Piping bag, 6 mm (¼ in) plain nozzle
- Rolling pin
- Baking tray (pan)
- Digital food thermometer
- Cling film (plastic wrap), baking parchment

FOR 1 SAINT-HONORÉ
- 55 g hazelnut sweet pastry
- 60 g vanilla crémeux
- 95 g vanilla Chantilly cream
- 15 g choux pastry
- 15 g caramel

FOR THE VANILLA CRÉMEUX
- 3 g leaf gelatine
- 1 vanilla pod
- 130 g cream (30% fat)
- 66 g egg yolks
- 31 g caster (superfine) sugar
- 115 g mascarpone

FOR THE HAZELNUT SWEET PASTRY
- 143 g plain (all-purpose) flour
- 34 g icing (powdered) sugar
- 22 g caster (superfine) sugar
- 22 g ground hazelnuts
- 79 g unsalted butter
- 31 g egg

FOR THE CHOUX PASTRY
- 20 g whole milk
- 20 g water
- 2 g inverted sugar
- 1 g salt
- 17 g unsalted butter
- 25 g plain (all-purpose) flour
- 35 g egg

FOR THE VANILLA CHANTILLY CREAM
- 519 g whipping cream (30% fat)
- 51 g caster (superfine) sugar
- 1 vanilla pod

FOR THE CARAMEL
- 22 g water
- 68 g caster (superfine) sugar

VANILLA SAINT-HONORÉS (cont.)

1. The day before, make the vanilla crémeux. Soak the gelatine in cold water. Split the vanilla pod and scrape out the seeds, then add both to the cream in a saucepan and bring to the boil. In a bowl, beat the egg yolks with the sugar until thick and pale. When the cream comes to the boil, remove from the heat and pour a little over the beaten yolk mixture, then return everything to the saucepan. Heat until the temperature of the mixture reaches 82°C (180°F). Lift the gelatine from the water, squeeze out any excess liquid, then stir into the crémeux until dissolved. Refrigerate for 24 hours.

2. On the day, make the sweet pastry. In the food processor, mix together the flour, icing sugar, caster sugar, ground hazelnuts and butter to very fine crumbs. Incorporate the egg. Shape the dough into a ball, wrap in cling film and refrigerate for 4 hours.

3. Preheat the oven to 160°C (325°F). Roll out the dough to a thickness of 3 mm (⅛ in) and cut out six 12 cm (4½ in) diameter discs. Grease the tart rings, then line them with the dough. Bake for 18–20 minutes. Allow to cool.

4. Make the choux pastry. In a saucepan, combine the milk, water, inverted sugar, salt and butter. Bring to the boil, then remove from the heat and whisk in the flour. Return to the heat and dry off the excess liquid by stirring constantly with a spatula. Transfer the pastry to a mixer fitted with a paddle and gradually incorporate the egg. Transfer the pastry to a piping bag and pipe 24 × 5 g (¼ oz) choux buns onto a baking tray (pan) lined with baking parchment.

5. Preheat the oven to 180°C (350°F). Bake for 12 minutes with the oven door slightly ajar.

6. After resting for 24 hours, put the crémeux into the mixer fitted with the whisk and add the mascarpone. Whisk until well combined and fluffy. It can be used immediately.

7. To make the vanilla Chantilly cream, combine the cream and sugar in the mixer. Split open the vanilla pod and scrape out the seeds with a knife. Add the seeds to the cream and whip to stiff peaks.

8. Fill each tart case with 25 g of vanilla crémeux. Then fill each tart case to the top with Chantilly cream, piping a swirl in the centre.

9. Put the rest of the crémeux into a piping bag, attach a small nozzle and fill the choux buns.

10. Make the caramel. In a saucepan, heat the water and sugar to a light caramel colour. Dip each choux bun into the caramel. When the caramel has set, arrange three choux buns evenly spaced around the Chantilly cream swirl on each tartlet. Pipe a little whipped cream between the choux buns. Pipe a swirl of Chantilly cream over everything and top with a final choux bun.

FIG TARTLETS

MAKES **6** ✦ PREPARATION TIME: **1 HR** ✦ COOKING TIME: **18–20 MINS** ✦ RESTING TIME: **6 HRS**

EQUIPMENT
- 6 tart rings, 8 cm (3 in) in diameter and 3 cm (1¼ in) deep
- Rolling pin
- Cling film (plastic wrap)

FOR 1 TARTLET
- 55g charcoal sweet pastry
- 30g almond cream
- 20g fig jam
- 60g fresh figs

FOR THE CHARCOAL SWEET PASTRY
- 142g plain (all-purpose) flour
- 33g icing (powdered) sugar
- 21g caster (superfine) sugar
- 21g ground hazelnuts
- 79g unsalted butter
- 3g food-grade activated charcoal
- 31g egg

FOR THE FIG JAM
- 98g fresh figs
- 22g caster (superfine) sugar

FOR THE ALMOND CREAM
- 45g unsalted butter, at room temperature
- 45g caster (superfine) sugar
- 45g ground almonds (almond flour)
- 45g egg

TO FINISH
- 360g fresh figs

1. Make the sweet pastry. Mix together the flour, icing sugar, caster sugar, ground hazelnuts and butter to very fine crumbs. Incorporate the charcoal and egg. Shape the dough into a ball, wrap in cling film and refrigerate for 4 hours.

2. Preheat the oven to 160°C (325°F). Roll out the dough to a thickness of 3 mm (⅛ in). Cut out six 12 cm (4½ in) diameter discs. Grease the tart rings, then line them with the dough. Bake for 18–20 minutes. Allow to cool.

3. Make the fig jam. Cut the figs into pieces and combine with the sugar in a saucepan. Cook over a low heat for 15–20 minutes.

4. Make the almond cream. Mix the softened butter with the sugar and ground almonds until smooth, then incorporate the egg.

5. Divide the almond cream into the tartlet cases, return them to the oven at 160°C (325°F) and bake until the almond cream colours, about 10 minutes. Allow to cool, then add the fig jam and smooth the surface. Arrange fresh fig pieces on each tartlet.

CHARCOAL-COCONUT SAINT-HONORÉS

MAKES **6** ✦ PREPARATION TIME: **2 HRS** ✦ COOKING TIME: **30–32 MINS** ✦ RESTING TIME: **24 HRS + 4 HRS**

EQUIPMENT
- 6 tart rings, 8 cm (3 in) in diameter and 3 cm (1¼ in) deep
- Food processor
- Stand mixer, whisk, paddle
- Hand-held blender
- Piping bag, 6 mm (¼ in) plain nozzle, star nozzle
- Rolling pin
- Baking tray (pan)
- Round pastry cutter, 2.5 cm (1 in) in diameter
- Digital food thermometer
- Cling film (plastic wrap), baking parchment

FOR 1 SAINT-HONORÉ
- 55g charcoal sweet pastry
- 73g charcoal craquelin
- 45g charcoal choux pastry
- 25g coconut-almond praline
- 60 g coconut crémeux
- 40g whipped coconut ganache

FOR THE WHIPPED COCONUT GANACHE
- 2g leaf gelatine
- 97g coconut milk
- 44g white chocolate
- 97g single (light) cream

FOR THE CHARCOAL SWEET PASTRY
- 142g plain (all-purpose) flour
- 33g icing (powdered) sugar
- 21g caster (superfine) sugar
- 21g ground hazelnuts
- 79g unsalted butter, diced
- 3g food-grade activated charcoal
- 31g egg

FOR THE CHARCOAL CRAQUELIN
- 21g unsalted butter
- 26g plain (all-purpose) flour
- 26g soft light brown sugar
- 1g food-grade activated charcoal

FOR THE CHARCOAL CHOUX PASTRY
- 20g whole milk
- 20g water
- 2g inverted sugar
- 1g salt
- 18g unsalted butter
- 24g plain (all-purpose) flour
- 2g food-grade activated charcoal
- 33g egg

FOR THE COCONUT CRÉMEUX
- 2g leaf gelatine
- 240g coconut milk
- 60g single (light) cream
- 27g egg yolks
- 27g caster (superfine) sugar

FOR THE COCONUT-ALMOND PRALINE
- 48g ground almonds
- 24g desiccated (shredded) coconut
- 16g water
- 48g caster (superfine) sugar
- 14g grapeseed oil

CHARCOAL-COCONUT **SAINT-HONORÉ** (cont.)

1. The day before, make the coconut ganache. Soak the gelatine in cold water. Heat the coconut milk in a saucepan. Pour it over the white chocolate, add the gelatine and stir until dissolved. Mix in the cream. Refrigerate for 24 hours.

2. On the day, make the sweet pastry. In the food processor, mix together the flour, icing sugar, caster sugar, ground hazelnuts and butter to very fine crumbs. Incorporate the charcoal and egg. Shape the dough into a ball, wrap in cling film and refrigerate for 4 hours

3. Preheat the oven to 160°C (325°F). Roll out the dough to a thickness of 3 mm (⅛ in). Cut out six 12 cm (4½ in) diameter discs. Grease the tart rings, then line them with the dough. Bake for 18–20 minutes. Allow to cool.

4. Make the craquelin. Put all the ingredients into the mixer fitted with the paddle and mix to a smooth paste. Using a rolling pin, roll out the paste as thinly as possible between two sheets of baking parchment. Using the pastry cutter, cut out at least 24 discs, each 2.5 cm (1 in) in diameter.

5. Make the choux pastry. In a saucepan, combine the milk, water, inverted sugar, salt and butter. Bring to the boil, then remove from the heat and incorporate the flour and charcoal with a spatula. Return to the heat and dry off the excess liquid by stirring constantly with the spatula. Transfer the pastry to a mixer fitted with a paddle and gradually incorporate the egg. Transfer the pastry to a piping bag and pipe at least 24 choux buns, each about 5 g, on a baking tray (pan) lined with baking parchment. Top each choux bun with a craquelin disc. Increase the oven temperature to 180°C (350°F). Bake for 10–12 minutes with the oven door slightly ajar.

6. Make the coconut crémeux. Soak the gelatine in cold water. Heat the coconut milk and cream in a saucepan. In a bowl, beat the egg yolks with the caster sugar until thick and pale. Add some of the hot liquid, then return everything to the saucepan and cook until the temperature reaches 85°C (185°F). Blend until smooth, then blend in the gelatine. Set aside.

7. Make the coconut-almond praline. Put the almonds and desiccated coconut on a baking tray lined with baking parchment and roast for a few minutes in the oven at 180°C (350°F). Allow to cool to room temperature. In a saucepan, heat the water and sugar to make a light caramel. Add the almonds and coconut and mix well. Allow to cool, then blend, gradually adding the oil, to form a paste.

8. Fill the tart cases with the praline. Fill the choux buns with coconut crémeux and use the remainder to fill the tartlet cases to the top. Smooth the surface.

9. In the mixer fitted with the whisk, whip the ganache until it is creamy and stands upright on the whisk. Put the ganache into a piping bag and attach the star nozzle. Pipe a swirl of ganache in the centre each tartlet. Arrange three choux buns, evenly spaced, around the ganache. Pipe ganache between the choux buns. Pipe a swirl in the centre and top with a final choux bun.

RASPBERRY & POPPY SEED **PAVLOVAS**

MAKES **6** ✦ PREPARATION TIME: **1 HR** ✦ COOKING TIME: **3 HRS 20 MINS** ✦ RESTING TIME: **4 HRS**

EQUIPMENT
- 6 tart rings, 8 cm (3 in) in diameter and 3 cm (1¼ in) deep
- Piping bag, plain nozzle
- Stand mixer, whisk
- Baking tray (pan)
- Hand whisk
- Rolling pin
- Cling film (plastic wrap)

FOR 1 PAVLOVA
- 55g charcoal sweet pastry
- 29g poppy seed Chantilly cream
- 30g raspberry jam
- 35g fresh raspberries
- 20g meringue

FOR THE MERINGUE
- 48g egg whites
- 48g caster (superfine) sugar
- 24g icing (powdered) sugar
- A handful poppy seeds

FOR THE CHARCOAL SWEET PASTRY
- 142g plain (all-purpose) flour
- 33g icing (powdered) sugar
- 21g caster (superfine) sugar
- 21g ground hazelnuts
- 79g unsalted butter
- 30g egg
- 3g food-grade activated charcoal

FOR THE RASPBERRY JAM
- 142g raspberry purée
- 24g lemon juice
- 43g caster (superfine) sugar
- 2g pectin NH

FOR THE POPPY SEED CHANTILLY CREAM
- 153g whipping cream (30% fat)
- 15g caster (superfine) sugar
- 6g poppy seeds

TO FINISH
- 210g fresh raspberries

1. Preheat the oven to 70°C (160°F). Make the meringue. Combine all the ingredients, except the poppy seeds, in a stand mixer fitted with a whisk and beat on the highest speed to soft peaks. Transfer the meringue to a piping bag and pipe 6 small mounds 8 cm (3 in) in diameter on a baking tray (pan) lined with baking parchment. Sprinkle with the poppy seeds and bake for 3 hours with the oven door slightly ajar.

2. Make the sweet pastry. Mix together the flour, icing sugar, caster sugar, ground hazelnuts and butter to very fine crumbs. Incorporate the egg and charcoal. Shape the dough into a ball, wrap in cling film and refrigerate for 4 hours.

3. Preheat the oven to 160°C (325°F). Roll out the dough to a thickness of 3 mm (⅛ in). Cut out six 12 cm (4½ in) diameter discs. Grease the tart rings, then line them with the dough. Bake for 18–20 minutes. Allow to cool.

4. Make the raspberry jam. In a saucepan, heat the raspberry purée and lemon juice to 45°C (113°F). Mix the sugar with the pectin, add to the mixture in the saucepan and bring to the boil for 12 seconds. Allow to cool, then strain and refrigerate.

5. Make the Chantilly cream. Using the hand whisk, whip the cream with the sugar and incorporate the poppy seeds at the end.

6. Transfer the whipped cream to a piping bag and fill the tartlet cases three-quarters full. Fill the remainder with raspberry jam and smooth the surface. Arrange the fresh raspberries over the tartlets, pipe a dot of Chantilly cream in the centre of each one and carefully cover with a meringue.

Tip
If the jam is too firm, loosen it with a whisk before use.

TONKA BEAN & CHOCOLATE **PAVLOVAS**

MAKES **6** ✦ PREPARATION TIME: **1 HR** ✦ COOKING TIME: **3 HRS 20 MINS** ✦ RESTING TIME: **24 HRS + 4 HRS**

EQUIPMENT
- 6 tart rings, 8 cm (3 in) in diameter and 3 cm (1¼ in) deep
- Piping bag, plain nozzle
- Hand whisk
- Stand mixer, whisk
- Rolling pin
- Conical sieve
- Cling film (plastic wrap), baking parchment

FOR 1 PAVLOVA TARTLET
- 55g chocolate sweet pastry
- 50g milk chocolate Chantilly cream
- 20g chocolate-tonka bean caramel sauce
- 20g namelaka
- 20g cocoa meringue

FOR THE NAMELAKA
- 37g milk chocolate (45% cocoa)
- 2g glucose
- 27g whole milk
- 54g whipping cream (35% fat)

FOR THE MILK CHOCOLATE CHANTILLY CREAM
- 100g milk chocolate (45% cocoa)
- 200g whipping cream (30% fat)

FOR THE COCOA SWEET PASTRY
- 135g plain (all-purpose) flour
- 67g icing (powdered) sugar
- 1g salt
- 16g cocoa powder
- 67g unsalted butter
- 24g egg yolks
- 20g egg

FOR THE CHOCOLATE-TONKA BEAN CARAMEL SAUCE
- 12g sugar
- 14g + 6g glucose
- 33g cream
- 12g + 13g whole milk
- 4g cocoa powder
- 1g ground tonka bean
- 6g milk chocolate (45% cocoa)
- 6g dark chocolate (59% cocoa)
- 13g unsalted butter

FOR THE COCOA MERINGUE
- 47g egg whites
- 47g caster (superfine) sugar
- 24g icing (powdered) sugar
- 2g cocoa powder

TONKA BEAN & CHOCOLATE **PAVLOVAS** (cont.)

1. The day before, make the namelaka. In a heatproof bowl set over a pan of simmering water, melt the chocolate, then add the glucose. Bring the milk to the boil and pour it over the chocolate. Add the well-chilled cream and blend until smooth. Refrigerate for 24 hours.

2. Make the Chantilly cream. Break the chocolate into pieces and put into a bowl. Pour the cream into a saucepan, bring to the boil, then pour it over the chocolate. Stir to combine, then whip using a hand whisk. Refrigerate for 24 hours.

3. On the day, make the sweet pastry. In a bowl, mix the flour with the icing sugar, salt and cocoa. Melt the butter and add it to the dry ingredients. Work the dough with your fingers. Add the egg yolks and continue to work the dough until its texture is fine and sandy. Shape the dough into a ball, wrap in cling film and refrigerate for 4 hours.

4. Preheat the oven to 160°C (325°F). Roll out the dough to a thickness of 3 mm (⅛ in) and cut out six 12 cm (4½ in) discs. Grease the tart rings, line with the dough and bake for 18–20 minutes. Allow to cool.

5. Make the caramel sauce. In a saucepan, heat the sugar and the 14 g of glucose to 185°C (365°C) to make a rich caramel. In a separate saucepan, heat the cream, the 12 g of milk, the 6 g of glucose and the cocoa. When the mixture comes to the boil, turn off the heat, add the ground tonka bean and allow to infuse for 20 minutes. Strain through a sieve, return to the pan and bring back to the boil. Deglaze the caramel with the cream mixture and heat to 105°C (221°F). Allow the mixture to cool to 70°C (158°F) before adding it to the milk and dark chocolate, cut into pieces in a bowl. Blend in the butter and the 13 g of milk. Transfer the sauce to a container and refrigerate.

6. Reduce the oven temperature to 70°C (160°F). Make the meringue. In the mixer fitted with the whisk, beat the eggs and sugar on the highest speed. When the meringue has an elastic consistency, transfer it to a piping bag and pipe six small mounds 8 cm (3 in) in diameter on a baking tray (pan) lined with baking parchment. Scatter with the cocoa. Bake for 3 hours with the oven door slightly ajar.

7. Assemble the tartlets. Partially fill the tartlet cases with caramel sauce and allow to set. Cover the caramel with namelaka, then refrigerate for 20–30 minutes to set the filling.

8. Fill the remainder with Chantilly cream and smooth the surface. Pipe small balls of Chantilly cream over the pastry sides and carefully top each tartlet with a meringue.

COCOA CHOUX PASTRY

MAKES **1 DESSERT FOR 6 PEOPLE** ✦ PREPARATION TIME: **25 MINS**
COOKING TIME: **10–12 MINS**

EQUIPMENT
- **Stand mixer, paddle**
- **Piping bag, star nozzle**
- **Baking tray (pan)**
- **Baking parchment**

FOR THE CHOUX PASTRY
- **60 g whole milk**
- **60 g water**
- **7 g inverted sugar**
- **3 g salt**
- **53 g unsalted butter**
- **72 g plain (all-purpose) flour**
- **5g cocoa powder**
- **106 g eggs**

1. In a saucepan, combine the milk, water, inverted sugar, salt and butter. Bring to the boil, then remove from the heat and whisk in the flour and cocoa until incorporated.

2. Return to the heat and dry off the excess liquid by stirring constantly with a spatula. Transfer the pastry to a mixer fitted with a paddle and gradually incorporate the eggs.

3. Transfer the choux pastry to a piping bag and pipe portions as required on a baking tray (pan) lined with baking parchment.

4. Preheat the oven to 180°C (325°F). Bake for 10–12 minutes, depending on the size of the pastries, leaving the oven door slightly ajar as they bake.

BASTARDS

PECAN **PARIS-BRESTS**

MAKES **6** ✦ PREPARATION TIME: **1 HR** ✦ COOKING TIME: **30 MINS** ✦ RESTING TIME: **24 HRS**

EQUIPMENT
- Stand mixer, paddle
- Blender
- Rolling pin
- Hand whisk
- Piping bag, star nozzle
- Baking tray (pan)
- Baking parchment

FOR 1 PARIS-BREST
- 50g cocoa choux pastry
- 8g cocoa craquelin
- 60g praline diplomat cream
- 20g pecan praline
- 3g pecan nuts

FOR THE COCOA CRAQUELIN
- 14g unsalted butter
- 14g plain (all-purpose) flour
- 18g soft light brown sugar
- 2g cocoa powder

FOR THE COCOA CHOUX PASTRY
- 50g whole milk
- 50g water
- 6g inverted sugar
- 2g salt
- 44g unsalted butter
- 56g plain (all-purpose) flour
- 4g cocoa powder
- 88g eggs

FOR THE PECAN PRALINE
- 84g caster (superfine) sugar
- 30g water
- 126g pecan nuts

FOR THE PRALINE DIPLOMAT CREAM
- 98g whole milk
- 8g custard powder
- 20g caster (superfine) sugar
- 20g egg yolk
- 120g pecan praline (see above)
- 17g unsalted butter
- 122g whipping cream (35% fat)

TO FINISH
- 18g pecan nuts

PECAN **PARIS-BRESTS** (cont.)

1. The day before, make the craquelin. Put all the ingredients into a mixer fitted with a paddle and mix to a smooth paste. Using a rolling pin, roll out the paste to a thickness of 2 mm (1⁄16 in) between 2 sheets of baking parchment. Cut out six rings about 10 cm (4 in) in diameter. Refrigerate for 24 hours.

2. On the day, make the choux pastry. In a saucepan, combine the milk, water, inverted sugar, salt and butter and bring to the boil. Remove from the heat and stir in the flour and cocoa. Return to the heat and dry off the excess liquid by stirring constantly with a spatula. Transfer the pastry to the mixer fitted with the paddle and incorporate the eggs. Transfer the pastry to a piping bag and pipe 6 rings about 10 cm (4 in) in diameter on a baking tray (pan) lined with baking parchment.

3. Preheat the oven to 180°C (350°F). Place a craquelin ring on top of each choux pastry ring and bake for 20 minutes. Reduce the oven temperature to 160°C (325°F) and bake for a further 10 minutes. Transfer to a rack and allow to cool.

4. Make the pecan praline. In a saucepan, make a caramel with the caster sugar and water. Pour the caramel over the pecans and allow to cool.Blend to a runny paste. Make the diplomat cream. In a saucepan, bring the milk to a boil. In a bowl, mix the custard powder with the sugar. Add the egg yolks to the dry ingredients and mix with a whisk until combined. Pour over part of the milk. Mix with a whisk, then pour back into the remaining milk in the saucepan. Bring to the boil for 1 minute, stirring constantly to keep the mixture from burning. Remove from the heat, stir in half the praline and the butter, then transfer to a bowl. Refrigerate until completely cool.

5. Whip the cream with the hand whisk and fold it into the cooled mixture. Transfer the diplomat cream to a piping bag fitted with a star nozzle.

6. Cut the choux pastry rings in half across the middle and cover the bottom halves with diplomat cream. Fill a piping bag with the remaining praline and pipe it over the diplomat cream, then cover with the top halves of the choux pastry rings.

7. Break the pecans into pieces and spread them over the sides of the Paris-Brest.

Tip

Before blending the praline, you can add 10% of its volume in neutral oil.

CHOCOLATE ÉCLAIRS

MAKES **6** ✦ PREPARATION TIME: **1 HR** ✦ COOKING TIME: **30 MINS** ✦ RESTING TIME: **24 HRS**

EQUIPMENT

- Stand mixer, paddle
- Hand-held mixer, hand whisk
- Rolling pin
- Digital food thermometer
- Piping bag, ribbon nozzle and star nozzle
- Baking parchment

FOR 1 ÉCLAIR

- 50g cocoa choux pastry
- 8g cocoa craquelin
- 40g chocolate diplomat cream
- 20g chocolate mirror glaze
- 3g chocolate shavings

FOR THE CHOCOLATE MIRROR GLAZE

- 1g leaf gelatine
- 31g whipping cream (30% fat)
- 46g caster (superfine) sugar
- 16g water
- 16g cocoa powder

FOR THE COCOA CRAQUELIN

- 14g unsalted butter
- 14g plain (all-purpose) flour
- 18g soft light brown sugar
- 2g cocoa powder

FOR THE COCOA CHOUX PASTRY

- 50g whole milk
- 50g water
- 6g inverted sugar
- 2g salt
- 44g unsalted butter
- 56g plain (all-purpose) flour
- 4g cocoa powder
- 88g eggs

FOR THE CHOCOLATE DIPLOMAT CREAM

- 77g whole milk
- 6g custard powder
- 15g caster (superfine) sugar
- 15g egg yolk
- 49g dark chocolate (64% cocoa)
- 77g whipping cream (35% fat)

TO FINISH

- 18g dark chocolate

CHOCOLATE **ÉCLAIRS** (cont.)

1. The day before, make the mirror glaze. Soak the gelatine in cold water. In a saucepan, bring the cream to the boil and set aside. In another saucepan, heat the sugar and water. Once the temperature reaches 105°C (221°F), stir in the cocoa. Deglaze the mixture with the still-hot cream. Add the gelatine and stir until dissolved. Blend until smooth. Transfer the glaze to a piping bag and refrigerate for 24 hours.

2. Next, make the craquelin. Put all the ingredients into a mixer fitted with a paddle and mix to a smooth paste. Using a rolling pin, roll out the paste to a thickness of 2 mm (1⁄16 in) between 2 sheets of baking parchment. Cut out six 14 × 3 cm (5½ × 1¼ in) strips. Refrigerate for 24 hours.

3. On the day, make the choux pastry. In a saucepan, combine the milk, water, inverted sugar, salt and butter and bring to the boil. Remove from the heat and incorporate the flour and cocoa. Return to the heat and dry off the excess liquid by stirring constantly with a spatula. Transfer the pastry to the mixer fitted with the paddle and gradually incorporate the eggs. Transfer the choux pastry to a piping bag fitted with a star nozzle and pipe 14 cm (5½ in) long éclairs on a baking tray (pan) lined with baking parchment.

4. Preheat the oven to 180°C (350°F). Lay a craquelin strip on top of each éclair and bake for 20 minutes. Reduce the oven temperature to 160°C (325°F) and bake for a further 10 minutes. Transfer to a rack and allow to cool.

5. Make the diplomat cream. In a saucepan, bring the milk to the boil. In a bowl, mix the custard powder with the sugar. Add the egg yolks to the dry ingredients and mix with a whisk until combined. Pour in part of the milk. Mix with a whisk, then pour back into the remaining milk in the saucepan. Bring to the boil for 30 seconds, stirring constantly. Remove from the heat and stir in the chocolate, then transfer to a bowl and refrigerate until completely cool.

6. Whip the cream with a hand whisk and fold it into the cooled mixture. Transfer the diplomat cream to a piping bag fitted with a nozzle.

7. Pierce a hole in the éclairs and fill them with the cream. Using the ribbon nozzle, pipe mirror glaze on the éclairs and grate chocolate over the top.

BAKED
BASTARDS

VANILLA TROPÉZIENNES

MAKES **6** ✦ PREPARATION TIME: **1 HR** ✦ COOKING TIME: **10–13 MINS** ✦ RESTING TIME: **OVERNIGHT + 1 HR**

EQUIPMENT
- Stand mixer, dough hook, paddle attachment
- Digital food thermometer
- Pastry brush
- Hand whisk, hand-held mixer
- Piping bags, nozzles
- Baking tray (pan)
- Baking parchment

FOR 1 TROPÉZIENNE
- 55 g charcoal brioche dough
- 10 g vanilla praline
- 50 g vanilla diplomat cream
- 10 g syrup, at 30°C (86°F)
- Pearl sugar

FOR THE CHARCOAL BRIOCHE DOUGH
- 105 g whole milk
- 29 g sunflower oil
- 155 g fine soft wheat flour (e.g., Italian 00 flour)
- 24 g caster (superfine) sugar
- 1 g salt
- 7 g bread improver
- 4 g food-grade activated charcoal
- 4 g yeast

FOR THE CHARCOAL ALMOND PRALINE
- 27 g almonds
- 18 g caster (superfine) sugar
- 6 g water
- 2 g food-grade activated charcoal

FOR THE VANILLA PRALINE
- 53 g charcoal almond praline
- 2 g vanilla bean paste
- 6 g whole milk

FOR THE VANILLA DIPLOMAT CREAM
- 150 g whole milk
- 1 vanilla pod
- 30 g caster (superfine) sugar
- 12 g custard powder
- 30 g egg yolk
- 78 g single (light) cream

FOR THE SYRUP
- 75 g water
- 75 g caster (superfine) sugar

VANILLA **TROPÉZIENNES** (cont.)

1. The day before, make the brioche dough. Combine the milk and oil in amixer fitted with a dough hook, then add the dry ingredients, adding the yeast last. Run the mixer to make a dough.

2. When the dough comes away from the sides of the bowl, stop the mixer and check the temperature, which should be 23–24°C (73–75°F). Transfer the dough to a container and refrigerate overnight.

3. On the day, divide the dough into six 55 g pieces. Allow the dough to rise at 28°C (82°F). In winter, place a container of hot water in a cold oven to heat it to this temperature. Once the brioche have doubled in size, preheat the oven to 160°C (325°F). Bake for 10–13 minutes, then allow to cool.

4. Make the charcoal almond praline. Place the almonds on a baking tray (pan) lined with baking parchment and lightly roast in the oven at 180°C (350°F). In a saucepan, heat the sugar, water and charcoal to 105°C (221°F). Add the still-warm almonds and stir to caramelise. Transfer to a baking tray lined with baking parchment and allow to cool, then blend to a paste.

5. Make the vanilla praline. Blend the charcoal almond praline with the vanilla bean paste and transfer to a bowl. Using a spatula, gently incorporate the milk a little at a time. Transfer to a piping bag.

6. Make the diplomat cream. Split the vanilla pod and scrape out the seeds. Add both the seeds and the pod to the milk in a saucepan and bring to the boil. In a bowl, mix the sugar and custard powder. Add the egg yolk to the dry ingredients and mix with a whisk until combined. Add a little of the boiling milk, mix and return the mixture to the pan with the remaining milk. Bring to the boil for 1 minute, stirring constantly to keep the cream from burning.

7. Using a hand whisk, whip the cream to stiff peaks. Loosen the pastry cream with a whisk before folding in the whipped cream. Transfer the diplomat cream to a piping bag and refrigerate for 1 hour.

8. To make the syrup, heat the sugar and water in a saucepan until dissolved.

9. When the brioche have cooled, cut them in half through the middle and brush the bottom halves with the syrup. Pipe a swirl of diplomat cream in the centre and spread vanilla praline over it. Pipe balls of diplomat cream over the edge of the base and cover with the top half of the brioches.

CHOCOLATE TROPÉZIENNES

MAKES **6** ✦ PREPARATION TIME: **1 HR** ✦ COOKING TIME: **10–15 MINS** ✦ RESTING TIME: **24 HRS + 1 HR**

EQUIPMENT
- Stand mixer, dough hook
- Hand-held mixer
- Hand whisk
- Piping bags, nozzle

FOR 1 TROPÉZIENNE
- 55g chocolate brioche dough
- 22g syrup
- 40g milk chocolate Chantilly cream
- 20g namelaka

FOR THE CHOCOLATE BRIOCHE DOUGH
- 128g pastry (sponge) flour
- 13g cocoa powder
- 76g eggs
- 3g salt
- 27g caster (superfine) sugar
- 15g whole milk
- 4g fresh yeast
- 64g unsalted butter

FOR THE CHOCOLATE WHIPPED CREAM
- 160g whipping cream (35% fat)
- 80g milk chocolate (45% cocoa)

FOR THE NAMELAKA
- 10 leaves gelatine
- 37g milk chocolate (45% cocoa)
- 2g glucose
- 27g whole milk
- 54g whipping cream (35% fat)

FOR THE SYRUP
- 45g caster (superfine) sugar
- 90g water

1. The day before, make the dough. In the mixer fitted with the dough hook, combine the flour, cocoa, eggs, salt, sugar, milk and yeast. Run the mixture to make a dough. When the dough comes away from the sides of the bowl, incorporate the butter. When it comes away again, transfer it to container and refrigerate overnight.

2. Next, prepare the chocolate cream for whipping. Bring the cream to the boil in a saucepan and pour it over the chocolate, broken into pieces in a bowl. Mix to combine, then blend. Refrigerate for 24 hours.

3. Next, make the namelaka. Soak the gelatine in cold water. In a heatproof bowl over a pan of simmering water, melt the chocolate and add the glucose. Bring the milk to the boil in a saucepan. Add the gelatine, stir to dissolve and add to the chocolate. Add the well-chilled cream and blend until smooth. Refrigerate for 24 hours.

4. On the day, divide the dough into six 55 g pieces and shape into 6 balls. Allow them to rise at 28°C (82°F). In winter, place a container of hot water in a cold oven to heat it to this temperature. Once the brioche have doubled in size, preheat the oven to 160°C (325°F). Bake for 10–15 minutes.

5. Make the syrup. Heat the sugar and water in a saucepan until dissolved.

6. Cut the brioche in half through the middle and brush the bottom halves with the syrup. Whip the chocolate cream with a hand whisk to a smooth consistency that will hold its shape when piped. Transfer to a piping bag, attach a nozzle and pipe balls in two rows around the edge of each brioche. Transfer the namelaka to a piping bag and fill the centre of the brioche before covering them with the top half.

CARAMEL-TONKA BEAN **TIRAMISU**

MAKES **6** ✦ PREPARATION TIME: **40 MINS** ✦ COOKING TIME: **10 MINS** ✦ RESTING TIME: **24 HRS**

EQUIPMENT
- **6 small dessert glasses**
- **Hand whisk**
- **Hand-held mixer**
- **Digital food thermometer**
- **Piping bag**
- **Baking tray (pan)**
- **Silicone spatula**
- **Baking parchment**

FOR 1 TIRAMISU
- **40 g sponge disc**
- **120 g tonka tiramisu cream**
- **20 g caramel sauce**
- **20 g syrup**
- **3 g chocolate shavings**

FOR THE CARAMEL SAUCE
- **20 g caster (superfine) sugar**
- **22 g + 10 g glucose**
- **42 g cream**
- **10 g whole milk**
- **15 g unsalted butter**

FOR THE SPONGE DISCS
- **74 g egg whites**
- **81 g caster (superfine) sugar**
- **36 g egg yolk**
- **35 g plain (all-purpose) flour**
- **15 g potato starch**

FOR THE TONKA TIRAMISU CREAM
- **34 g ground tonka beans**
- **286 g whipping cream (30% fat)**
- **286 g mascarpone**
- **58 g egg yolks**
- **58 g sugar**

FOR THE SYRUP
- **60 g caster (superfine) sugar**
- **60 g water**

TO FINISH
- **18 g dark chocolate**

1. The day before, add the ground tonka beans to the 286 g of cold cream and allow to infuse overnight.

2. Next, make the caramel sauce. In a saucepan, heat the sugar and the 22 g of glucose to 185°C (365°F). In a separate saucepan, heat the cream, milk and 10 g of glucose. When the caramel is at the right temperature, add it to the cream mixture and bring to the boil. Allow the mixture to cool to 70°C (158°F), then blend in the butter. Transfer to a piping bag and refrigerate for 24 hours.

3. On the day, make the tonka tiramisu cream. Using the hand whisk, whip the tonka-infused cream and mascarpone until light and fluffy. Whisk the egg yolks with the sugar until fluffy, then fold into the cream mixture. Refrigerate for a few minutes, then beat the mixture with the hand-held mixer until smooth and creamy.

4. Make the sponge. Preheat the oven to 190°C (375°F) and line a baking tray (pan) with baking parchment. Beat the egg whites until foamy, then add the sugar while continuing to beat. Incorporate the yolks. Using the silicone spatula, fold in the flour and potato starch to make a smooth batter. Spread the batter evenly in the baking tray and bake for 10 minutes.

5. To make the syrup, put the sugar and water into a saucepan and bring to the boil.

6. Take the sponge out of the oven and cut it into 12 discs the size of your glasses. Put a sponge disc in the bottom of each glass and soak it with the syrup. Pipe 20 g of caramel sauce into each glass, then add 60 g of tonka tiramisu cream. Place another sponge disc on top of the cream and soak it with syrup. Add a final layer of cream and grate chocolate over the top.

CARAMEL RICE PUDDING

SERVES **6** ✦ PREPARATION TIME: **30 MINS** ✦ COOKING TIME: **30 MINS** ✦ RESTING TIME: **24 HRS**

EQUIPMENT
- Hand-held blender
- Hand whisk
- Digital food thermometer
- Silicone spatula
- Baking tray (pan)
- Piping bag

FOR 1 PORTION
- 110g rice pudding
- 20g caramel sauce
- 8g hazelnut praline

FOR THE RICE PUDDING
- 443g whole milk
- 40g caster (superfine) sugar
- 2 vanilla pods
- 88g round-grain rice
- 88g whipping cream (30% fat)

FOR THE CARAMEL SAUCE
- 20g caster (superfine) sugar
- 22g + 10g glucose
- 42g whipping cream (30% fat)
- 10g whole milk
- 15g unsalted butter

FOR THE HAZELNUT PRALINE
- 25g hazelnuts
- 17g caster (superfine) sugar
- 6g water

1. The day before, make the caramel sauce. In a saucepan, heat the sugar and the 22 g of glucose to 185°C (365°F). In a separate saucepan, heat the cream, milk and 10 g of glucose. When the caramel is at the right temperature, add it to the cream mixture and bring to the boil. Allow the mixture to cool to 70°C (158°F), then blend in the butter. Refrigerate for 24 hours.

2. On the day, split the vanilla pods and scrape out the seeds. Put both in a saucepan with the milk and sugar. Add the rice and cook over a low heat to a creamy consistency. Stir the rice constantly and regularly with a spatula to keep it from sticking to the bottom of the pan and burning. Transfer the rice pudding to a bowl and allow to cool. Using the hand whisk, whip the cream and fold it into the cold rice pudding.

3. Place the hazelnuts on a baking tray (pan) and roast them for a few minutes in the oven at 180°C (330°F). In a saucepan, heat the sugar and water to 110°C (230°F), then add the roasted hazelnuts and stir to caramelise. Transfer to a shallow container.

4. Pipe the caramel sauce decoratively over the rice pudding, then scatter over with lightly crushed caramelised hazelnuts.

FOREST FRUIT & PISTACHIO **CRUMBLE**

SERVES **6** ✦ PREPARATION TIME: **30 MINS** ✦ COOKING TIME: **15–20 MINS**

EQUIPMENT
- **Stand mixer, paddle**
- **Ovenproof dish**

FOR THE BERRY COMPOTE
- **146g redcurrants (1)**
- **291g blueberries (1)**
- **291g raspberries (1)**
- **117g caster (superfine) sugar**
- **39g lemon juice**
- **48g redcurrants (2)**
- **146g blueberries (2)**
- **240g raspberries (2)**

FOR THE CRUMBLE TOPPING
- **250g pastry (sponge) flour**
- **125g caster (superfine) sugar**
- **125g soft light brown sugar**
- **250g unsalted butter**
- **250g ground pistachios**

1. In a saucepan, mix the first measures of fruit (1) with the sugar and lemon juice. Bring to the boil and simmer for 20 minutes. Allow to cool, then add the second measures of fruit (2). Mix, transfer to a container and set aside.

2. Make the crumble. Preheat the oven to 160°C (325°F). Put all the ingredients into the mixer fitted with the paddle attachment and mix to even crumbs.

3. Put the compote into the ovenproof dish. Spread the crumble over the fruit and bake for 15–20 minutes, until golden brown.

CARAMEL & POPCORN CHEESECAKE

SERVES **6** ✦ PREPARATION TIME: **30 MINS** ✦ COOKING TIME: **1 HR 20 MINS** ✦ RESTING TIME: **OVERNIGHT**

EQUIPMENT
- 22 cm (8½ in) pastry ring
- Stand mixer, paddle, whisk
- Rolling pin
- Baking tray (pan)
- Piping bag
- Baking parchment

FOR 1 CHEESECAKE, 22 CM IN DIAMETER
- 140 g biscuit base
- 1 kg cheesecake filling
- 240 g caramel sauce

FOR THE CARAMEL SAUCE
- 83 g whipping cream (30% fat)
- 56 g glucose
- 56 g caster (superfine) sugar
- 32 g unsalted butter
- 14 g cocoa butter
- 1 g salt

FOR THE SPECULOOS BISCUIT
- 42 g plain (all-purpose) flour
- 1 g baking powder
- 21 g unsalted butter
- 11 g vergoise blonde (light caramelised sugar)
- 11 g muscovado sugar
- 6 g caster (superfine) sugar
- 1 g cinnamon
- 6 g egg
- 4 g whole milk

FOR THE BISCUIT BASE
- 100 g speculoos biscuit (see above)
- 40 g unsalted butter, melted

FOR THE CHEESECAKE FILLING
- 580 g Philadelphia® cream cheese
- 171 g caster (superfine) sugar
- 28 g plain (all-purpose) flour
- 154 g eggs
- 33 g egg yolk
- 34 g whipping cream (35% fat)

TO FINISH
- 2 large handfuls of popcorn

CARAMEL & POPCORN **CHEESECAKE** (cont.)

1. Make the cheesecake and caramel sauce the day before so they can rest overnight. Start by making the caramel sauce. Heat the cream in a saucepan. In a separate saucepan, heat the glucose and sugar to a rich caramel. Mix in the hot cream. Heat the butter and cocoa butter to 70°C (158°F) and incorporate it into the sauce. Add the salt. Transfer to a container and refrigerate overnight.

2. Next, make the biscuit. Preheat the oven to 170°C (340°F). Sift the flour with the baking powder. In the mixer fitted with the paddle, mix the butter with the sugars and cinnamon, then add the egg and milk. Incorporate the dry ingredients to make a dough. Roll out the dough to a thickness of 3 mm (⅛ in) and place on a baking tray (pan) lined with baking parchment. Bake for 12–15 minutes.

3. To make the base, put the baked biscuit into the mixer fitted with the paddle and run the mixer until large crumbs form. Add the melted butter to the crumbs and mix until smooth.

4. Press the biscuit base into the pastry ring. Bake for 7 minutes at 170°C (340°F).

5. Make the filling. In the mixer fitted with the whisk, mix together the cream cheese, sugar and flour. Gradually mix in the eggs, egg yolk and cream.

6. Lower the oven temperature to 90°C (195°F). Fill the ring to the brim with the filling mixture and bake for 1 hour.

7. Refrigerate overnight.

8. On the day, put the caramel sauce into a piping bag and cover the top of the cheesecake. Scatter popcorn over the top before serving.

BÂTARD
FRENCH TOAST

SERVES **6** ✦ PREPARATION TIME: **1 HR** ✦ COOKING TIME: **30 MINS** ✦ RESTING TIME: **1 HR 35 MINS**

EQUIPMENT
- **Stand mixer, dough hook**
- **Rolling pin**
- **Loaf tin (pan)**
- **Pastry brush**

FOR THE SANDWICH BREAD
- **80 g water**
- **80 g whole milk**
- **50 g egg**
- **4 g salt**
- **250 g plain (all-purpose) flour**
- **25 g caster (superfine) sugar**
- **3 g fresh yeast**
- **15 g unsalted butter**

FOR THE SOAKING MIXTURE
- **1.5 litres whole milk**
- **500 g whipping cream (30% fat)**
- **120 g egg yolks**
- **200 g whole eggs**
- **500 g caster (superfine) sugar**

TO FINISH
- **1 egg, for glazing**
- **Butter**

1. Start by making the bread. In the mixer fitted with the dough hook, combine the water, milk and egg. Add the salt, flour, sugar and yeast (add the yeast last because it must not be in contact with the salt). Mix for 4 minutes on the lowest speed to form a dough, then add the butter, cut into pieces. Increase the speed to high and knead for 6 minutes. The butter should be perfectly incorporated and the dough smooth. When the dough comes away from the sides of the bowl, transfer to a greased bowl, cover with a cloth and rest for 45 minutes at room temperature.

2. Transfer the dough to a greased or floured work surface and divide it into two 250 g pieces. Cover with a cloth and rest for a further 10 minutes.

3. Using the rolling pin, deflate each piece of dough while rolling it out into a rectangle. Roll up each rectangle into a sausage. Grease the loaf tin (pan) and place the two sausages side by side lengthways inside. Cover with a cloth and prove for 45 minutes at room temperature. You can find step-by-step instructions and photographs on pages 158–159.

4. Preheat the oven to 180°C (350°F). The dough should have risen to the top of the tin. Brush the top of the dough with the beaten egg and bake for 25 minutes.

5. Turn the loaf out of the tin and return it to the oven to bake for a further 5 minutes. Allow to cool on a rack.

6. Make the soaking mixture. Mix all the cold ingredients and set aside in the refrigerator.

7. When the bread has cooled, cut it into 2 cm (1¾ in) thick slices. Cover them completely with plenty of soaking mixture and allow to soak for 5–10 minutes.

8. Melt the butter in a frying pan and toast the soaked bread slices over a medium heat for 4–5 minutes on each side, until golden brown.

Tip
You can coat the French toast with chocolate and hazelnut spread (see page 16) before serving.

CHOCOLATE MARBLE CAKE

SERVES **6** ✦ PREPARATION TIME: **30 MINS** ✦ COOKING TIME: **30 MINS**

EQUIPMENT
- **450 g loaf tin (pan)**
- **Stand mixer, paddle, whisk**
- **Piping bags**
- **Pastry brush**

FOR THE PLAIN CAKE BATTER
- **23g unsalted butter**
- **77g caster (superfine) sugar**
- **55g egg**
- **1g salt**
- **60g plain (all-purpose) flour**
- **2g baking powder**
- **32g single (light) cream**

FOR THE CHOCOLATE CAKE BATTER
- **23g unsalted butter**
- **77g caster (superfine) sugar**
- **55g egg**
- **1g salt**
- **57g plain (all-purpose) flour**
- **2g baking powder**
- **3g cocoa powder**
- **32g single (light) cream**

FOR THE TOPPING
- **75g dark chocolate (55% cocoa)**
- **225g dark compound chocolate**
- **38g grapeseed oil**
- **a handful hazelnuts**

1. Put all the butter into the mixer fitted with the paddle and beat until soft. Set aside a small amount for finishing.

2. Make the plain cake batter. In the mixer fitted with the whisk, beat the sugar with the eggs for 2 minutes. Add the salt, flour and baking powder. Mix on low-medium speed for 2 minutes, then incorporate half the softened butter and the cream.

3. To make the chocolate cake batter, repeat the process for the plain batter but add the cocoa at the same time as the flour.

4. Fill separate piping bags with the different batters. Preheat the oven to 180°C (350°F). Grease and flour the loaf tin (pan). Pipe alternating layers of cake batter inside the tin. Pass a knife back and forth through the batter to create a marbled effect. Pipe a line of softened butter along the length of the cake for a well-formed crack.

5. Bake for 20 minutes, then lower the oven temperature to 160°C (325°F) and bake for a further 10 minutes.

6. Turn out the cake onto a wire rack and allow to cool.

7. Meanwhile, make the icing. Melt the chocolates in a bowl set over a pan of simmering water. Stir in the oil.

8. Using the pastry brush, cover the cold cake with the topping and scatter with the hazelnuts.

BANANA & MAPLE SYRUP CAKE WITH CHOCOLATE ICING

SERVES **6** ✦ PREPARATION TIME: **30 MINS** ✦ COOKING TIME: **30 MINS**

EQUIPMENT
- **450 g loaf tin (pan)**
- **Stand mixer, paddle, whisk**
- **Hand-held mixer**
- **Piping bag**

FOR THE CAKE BATTER
- **128g banana**
- **69g unsalted butter**
- **128g caster (superfine) sugar**
- **78g eggs**
- **93g plain (all-purpose) flour**
- **4g baking powder**

FOR THE SYRUP
- **300g water**
- **60g maple syrup**

FOR THE CHOCOLATE ICING
- **246g milk chocolate (45% cocoa solids)**
- **25g cocoa butter**
- **65g finely chopped hazelnuts**

1. Make the cake batter. Purée the banana. Put the butter into the mixer fitted with the paddle and beat until soft. Set aside.

2. Fit the whisk to the mixer and beat the sugar with the eggs for 2 minutes. Mash the banana and add with the flour and baking powder. Mix on low-medium speed for 2 minutes, then incorporate the softened butter reserving a small amount for finishing.

3. Preheat the oven to 180°C (350°F). Grease and flour the loaf tin (pan). Fill with the batter and pipe a line of softened butter along the length of the cake for a well-formed crack.

4. Bake for 20 minutes, then lower the oven temperature to 140°C (280°F) and bake for a further 10 minutes.

5. Meanwhile, make the syrup. In a saucepan, combine the water and maple syrup and bring to the boil.

6. Turn out the cake onto a wire rack, soak with the syrup and allow to cool.

7. In a heatproof bowl over a pan of simmering water, melt the chocolate and cocoa butter, then add the chopped hazelnuts and mix well. Ice the cake.

LEMON **CAKE**

SERVES **6** ✦ PREPARATION TIME: **40 MINS** ✦ COOKING TIME: **30 MINS**

EQUIPMENT
- **450g loaf tin (pan)**
- **Stand mixer, paddle, whisk**
- **Piping bag**
- **Pastry brush**

FOR THE CAKE BATTER
- **42g unsalted butter**
- **160g caster (superfine) sugar**
- **105g eggs**
- **1g salt**
- **117g plain (all-purpose) flour**
- **2g baking powder**
- **63g single (light) cream**
- **5g lemon zest**
- **5g lemon juice**

FOR THE ICING
- **75g lemon juice**
- **300g icing (powdered) sugar**

1. Make the cake batter. Put the butter into the mixer fitted with the paddle and beat until soft. Set aside.

2. Fit the whisk to the mixer and beat the sugar with the eggs for 10 minutes. Add the salt, flour and baking powder. Mix on low-medium speed for 2 minutes, then incorporate the softened butter (setting aside a small amount for later), cream and lemon zest and juice.

3. Preheat the oven to 180°C (350°F). Grease and flour the loaf tin (pan). Fill with the batter and then pipe a line of softened butter along the length of the cake for a well-formed crack. Bake for 20 minutes, then lower the oven temperature to 160°C (325°F) and bake for a further 10 minutes. Turn out the cake onto a wire rack and allow to cool.

4. Make the icing by mixing the icing sugar with the lemon juice to a smooth paste.

5. Using the pastry brush, cover the cooled cake with the icing and place the cake in the oven for 1 minute at 90°C (195°F).

CHESTNUT **CAKE**

SERVES **6** ✦ PREPARATION TIME: **30 MINS** ✦ COOKING TIME: **30 MINS**

EQUIPMENT
- 450 g loaf tin (pan)
- Stand mixer, paddle, whisk
- Piping bag

FOR THE CAKE BATTER
- 40g unsalted butter
- 145g caster (superfine) sugar
- 95g eggs
- 1g salt
- 110g plain (all-purpose) flour
- 2g baking powder
- 22g chestnut paste
- 25g chestnut spread
- 60g single (light) cream

FOR THE CHESTNUT VERMICELLI
- 50g chestnut paste
- 50g chestnut spread
- 50g whipping cream (35% fat)

TO FINISH
- 30g marron glacé pieces

1. Make the cake batter. Put the butter into the mixer fitted with the paddle and beat until soft. Set aside.

2. Fit the whisk to the mixer and beat the sugar with the eggs for 2 minutes. Add the salt, flour and baking powder. Add the chestnut paste and spread. Mix on speed 2 for 2 minutes, then incorporate the softened butter (setting aside a small amount for later) and cream.

3. Preheat the oven to 180°C (350°F). Grease and flour the loaf tin (pan). Fill with the batter and pipe a line of softened butter along the length of the cake for a well-formed crack. Bake for 20 minutes, then lower the oven temperature to 140°C (280°F) and bake for a further 10 minutes. Allow to cool.

4. Make the chestnut vermicelli. Using the mixer fitted with the whisk, loosen the chestnut paste. Add the chestnut spread and mix until smooth, then incorporate the cream. Transfer the mixture to a piping bag.

5. Pipe thin strings of the chestnut mixture over the cake and decorate with marron glacé pieces.

03

BREAI
SAVO

OS &
URIES

FOCACCIA

SERVES **6** ✦ PREPARATION TIME: **30 MINS** ✦ COOKING TIME: **20–22 MINS** ✦ RESTING TIME: **3 HRS**

EQUIPMENT
- **24 × 30 × 6 cm (9½ × 12 × 2½ in) baking tin (pan)**
- **Stand mixer, dough hook, paddle**

FOR THE FOCACCIA DOUGH
- **847g strong white flour**
- **237g liquid sourdough starter**
- **17g salt**
- **4g fresh yeast**
- **525g cold water**
- **169g olive oil**

TO FINISH
- **Oil**
- **10 g flaked sea salt**
- **10g Espelette pepper**

1. Put the ingredients for the dough into the mixer fitted with the dough hook. Start mixing on the lowest speed for 4 minutes until a dough forms.

2. Replace the dough hook with the paddle and start kneading. Run the mixer on the lowest speed for 6 minutes, then on low-medium for 1 minute. Rest the dough at room temperature for 30 minutes.

3. After resting, knead the dough for 5 seconds on low speed. Transfer the dough to the oil-greased baking tin (pan) and rest for 1 hour.

4. Oil your fingers, then press them into the dough making regularly spaced dimples. Allow to prove for 1 hour 30 minutes.

5. Preheat the oven to 200°C (400°F) and place a pan of water inside, then bake the focaccia for 20–22 minutes.

6. Drizzle the focaccia with oil and scatter with flaked sea salt and the spice.

FOCACCIA WITH TOPPING

SERVES **6** ✦ PREPARATION TIME: **30 MINS** ✦ COOKING TIME: **20–22 MINS** ✦ RESTING TIME: **3 HRS + OVERNIGHT FOR THE PICKLES**

EQUIPMENT
- **24 × 30 × 6 cm (9½ × 12 × 2½ in) baking tin (pan)**
- **Stand mixer, dough hook, paddle**
- **Blender**
- **1 large glass Kilner or Mason jar**

FOR THE PICKLED CHERRY TOMATOES
- **400g cherry tomatoes**
- **2 cloves garlic**
- **1 sprig rosemary**
- **250g vinegar**
- **125g sugar**

FOR THE FOCACCIA
- **1.8 kg focaccia dough (see previous recipe)**
- **300g Bellocq® ham, sliced**
- **80g rocket (arugula)**
- **375g mozzarella**

FOR 381G PESTO
- **31g Parmesan**
- **2g garlic**
- **25g basil leaves**
- **34g pine nuts**
- **99g olive oil**
- **189g mascarpone**
- **10g salt**
- **Salt and pepper**

1. Make the pickled tomatoes. Sterilise the jar by boiling it in water for 15 minutes. Peel and thinly slice the garlic. Layer the tomatoes in the jar with the garlic and add the rosemary. Combine the vinegar and sugar in a saucepan, bring to the boil and pour into the jar. Seal the jar and allow to pickle over night at room temperature.

2. Put the focaccia dough into the oil-greased baking tin (pan) and rest for 1 hour. Oil your fingers and press them into the dough making regularly spaced dimples. Allow to prove for 1 hour 30 minutes.

3. Make the pesto. Grate the Parmesan. Peel, halve and degerm the garlic. Blend the basil with the garlic and pine nuts. Add the Parmesan and olive oil and blend for a few more seconds. Add the mascarpone and salt and season with pepper to taste.

4. Preheat the oven to 200°C (400°F) and place a pan of water inside, then bake the focaccia for 20–22 minutes.

5. Turn out the focaccia and allow to cool completely before spreading it with the pesto and adding the pickled cherry tomatoes. Finally, arrange the rocket, mozzarella and ham slices over the top.

BRIOCHE PIZZA

MAKES **6** ✦ PREPARATION TIME: **1 HR** ✦ COOKING TIME: **20 MINS** ✦ RESTING TIME: **24 HRS + 1 HR**

EQUIPMENT
- 14 cm (5½ in) stainless steel pastry ring
- Stand mixer, dough hook
- Blender
- Rolling pin
- Baking tray (pan)
- Angled palette knife
- Pastry brush
- Baking parchment

FOR 1 BRIOCHE PIZZA
- 200g brioche dough
- 133g tomato tapenade
- 140g roasted vegetables
- 100g pizza cheese
- 50g ricotta
- 20g mixed salad leaves
- Olive oil

FOR THE BRIOCHE DOUGH
- 500g pastry (sponge) flour
- 300g eggs
- 10g salt
- 105g caster (superfine) sugar
- 20g whole milk
- 15g fresh yeast
- 250g unsalted butter

FOR ROASTED VEGETABLES
- 400g aubergines
- 400g mushrooms
- 40g olive oil
- 10g paprika

FOR THE TOMATO TAPENADE
- 500g sun-dried tomatoes
- 100g fresh tomatoes
- 100g olive oil
- 30 g herbes de Provence
- 30g lemon juice
- 40g tomato purée (paste)

1. The day before, make the dough. In the mixer fitted with the dough hook, add the flour, eggs, salt, sugar, milk and yeast. Mix to a dough, then knead. When the dough comes away from the sides of the bowl, incorporate the butter. When it comes away again, transfer it to container and refrigerate overnight.

2. Prepare and roast the vegetables. Preheat the oven to 180°C (350°F). Wash and dice the aubergines and mushrooms. In an ovenproof dish, toss the vegetables with the olive oil and paprika. Roast for 25 minutes.

3. Make the tomato tapenade. Combine all the ingredients in the blender and blend to a paste. Transfer to a container and use immediately or store in the refrigerator.

4. Roll out the dough to a thickness of 4 mm (¼ in). Using the pastry ring as a template, cut out six 14 cm (5½ in) discs and lay them on a baking tray (pan) lined with baking parchment. Spread each brioche disc with tapenade. Top with the roasted vegetables and pizza cheese. Allow the dough to rise for 1 hour.

5. Preheat the oven to 160°C (325°F). Bake for 20 minutes.

6. Add the ricotta to the pizzas when they come out of the oven. Just before serving, drizzle with olive oil and arrange mixed salad leaves over the top.

TZATZIKI & ROAST TURKEY CROISSANTS

MAKES **6** ✦ PREPARATION TIME: **1 HR 20 MINS** ✦ COOKING TIME: **1 HR** ✦ RESTING TIME: **2 HRS 15 MINS**

EQUIPMENT
- Stand mixer, dough hook
- Baking tray (pan)
- Rolling pin
- Cling film (plastic wrap)

FOR 1 CROISSANT
- 100g croissant dough
- 116 g tzatziki
- 100g roast turkey
- 20g Little Gem lettuce
- Olive oil

FOR THE CROISSANT DOUGH
- 128g pastry (sponge) flour
- 128g fine soft wheat flour (e.g., Italian 00 flour)
- 5g salt
- 10g fresh yeast
- 12g unsalted butter, chilled
- 38g caster (superfine) sugar
- 7g cold water
- 105g whole milk, cold
- 13g egg
- 154g unsalted dry butter (84% fat)

FOR THE ROAST TURKEY
- 500g boneless turkey breast
- 60g olive oil
- 20g shallot
- 20g garlic

FOR THE TZATZIKI
- 200g cucumber
- 400g Greek yogurt
- 10g salt
- 40g lemon juice
- 10g garlic
- 30g olive oil
- 10g fresh mint

1. Make the croissants. In the mixer fitted with the dough hook, combine all the ingredients for the dough, except the dry butter. Mix for 5 minutes on the lowest speed to form a dough. Set the mixer to speed 2 and knead for 8 minutes. The dough should be smooth.

2. Shape the dough into a rectangle on a baking tray (pan) lined with baking parchment. Cover with cling film (plastic wrap), allowing it to be in direct contact with the dough, and rest for 15 minutes in the refrigerator.

3. Take the dough out of the refrigerator and use it to encase the dry butter. Make a double turn and roll out the dough to a thickness of 8 mm (⅓ in). Next, make a simple turn and roll it out to a thickness of 8 mm (⅓ in). Now roll out the dough to a thickness of 4 mm (¼ in). Follow the step-by-step instructions and photographs on pages 152–153 as a guide, as the same technique for folding and turning dough is used.

4. Cut out six triangles measuring 9 cm (½ in) wide at the base and 29 cm (11½ in) long (each should weigh 100 g). Starting at the widest part, roll the triangles into croissants.

5. Lay the croissants on a baking tray lined with baking parchment and allow to rise for 2 hours.

6. Meanwhile, roast the turkey. Preheat the oven to 180°C (350°F). Place the turkey in an ovenproof dish and smear the meat with olive oil. Peel and thinly slice the shallot and garlic, then add them to the bottom of the dish with a little water. Roast the turkey for 40 minutes, then very thinly slice.

7. Make the tzatziki. Peel, halve and deseed the cucumber, then finely grate and allow to drain in a sieve. Whisk together the remaining ingredients. Stir in the cucumber and refrigerate until ready to use.

8. When the croissants have doubled in size, preheat the oven to 150°C (300°F) and bake for 20 minutes. Allow to cool.

9. Slice open each croissant and spread some tzatziki inside. Add roast turkey slices. Separate the lettuce leaves, dress with a little olive oil and add to the croissants.

PASTRAMI, BÉCHAMEL & MIMOLETTE CRUFFINS

MAKES **6** ✦ PREPARATION TIME: **1 HR** ✦ COOKING TIME: **20–25 MINS** ✦ RESTING TIME: **2 HRS 15 MINS**

EQUIPMENT
- 6 round moulds, 9 cm (3½ in) in diameter and 4 cm (1½ in) deep
- Stand mixer, dough hook
- Hand-held mixer
- Hand whisk
- Baking tray (pan)
- Digital food thermometer
- Rolling pin
- Piping bag
- Cling film (plastic wrap)

FOR 1 CRUFFIN
- 100g croissant dough
- 100 g pastrami
- 100 g mimolette béchamel sauce
- 17g mimolette cheese

FOR THE CROISSANT DOUGH
- 128g pastry (sponge) flour
- 128g fine soft wheat flour (e.g., Italian 00 flour)
- 5g salt
- 10g fresh yeast
- 12g unsalted butter
- 38g caster (superfine) sugar
- 7g cold water
- 106g whole milk, cold
- 13g egg
- 154g unsalted dry butter (84% fat)

FOR THE MIMOLETTE BÉCHAMEL SAUCE
- 100g unsalted butter
- 100g plain (all-purpose) flour
- 200g whole milk
- 10g salt
- 10g pepper
- 180g mimolette cheese, grated

1. Make the croissants. In the mixer fitted with the dough hook, combine all the ingredients for the dough, except the dry butter. Mix for 5 minutes on the lowest speed to form a dough. Set the mixer to low-medium speed and knead for 8 minutes. The dough should be smooth.

2. Shape the dough into a rectangle on a baking tray (pan) lined with baking parchment. Cover with cling film (plastic wrap), allowing it to be in direct contact with the dough, and rest for 10–15 minutes in the refrigerator.

3. Take the dough out of the refrigerator and encase the dry butter. Make a double turn and roll out the dough to a thickness of 8 mm (⅓ in). Next, make a simple turn and roll it out to a thickness of 8 mm (⅓ in). Now roll out the dough to a thickness of 4 mm (⅛ in) with a width of 35 cm (13½ in). At the top and bottom of the dough, across the width, mark out six 4.5 cm (1¾ in) wide strips, then cut them out. Roll up the strips without pressing on the edges to allow the layers to separate. Follow the step-by-step instructions and photographs on pages 152–153 as a guide, as the same technique for folding and turning dough is used.

4. Arrange in the moulds and allow to rise for 2 hours, until doubled in size.

5. Preheat the oven to 150°C (300°F) and bake for 20–25 minutes. Allow to cool.

6. Make the béchamel sauce. Melt the butter in a saucepan, then remove from the heat and incorporate the flour to form a roux. Return the saucepan to a low heat and stir the roux constantly until thick, without colouring. Stir in the milk until combined. Add the salt, pepper and cheese, stirring regularly. When the cheese melts, transfer the béchamel sauce to a bowl and use immediately or store in the refrigerator.

7. Cut the cruffins in half across the middle and fill with béchamel sauce and pastrami. Add a little béchamel sauce to the top of the cruffins and sprinkle with grated cheese. Return the cruffins to the oven at 180°C (350°F) for 7 minutes.

CHALLAH

MAKES **6** ✦ PREPARATION TIME: **30 MINS** ✦ COOKING TIME: **17–20 MINS** ✦ RESTING TIME: **12 HRS + 1 HR 15 MINS**

EQUIPMENT
- **Stand mixer, paddle**
- **Digital food thermometer**

FOR THE CHALLAH DOUGH
- **596 g whole milk**
- **165 g sunflower oil**
- **870 g fine soft wheat flour (e.g., Italian 00 flour)**
- **7 g salt**
- **139 g caster (superfine) sugar**
- **23 g fresh yeast**

TO FINISH
- **1 egg, for glazing**
- **10 g sesame seeds**
- **10 g poppy seeds**

1. The day before, make the dough. Combine the milk and oil in the mixer fitted with the dough hook, followed by the dry ingredients. Add the yeast last. Run the mixer on speed 2. When the dough comes away from the sides of the bowl, stop the mixer and check the temperature, which should be 23–24°C (73–75°F). Transfer the dough to a container.

2. Refrigerate the dough overnight.

3. On the day, divide the dough into eighteen 100 g pieces and rest for 15 minutes. Shape each piece of dough into sausages 20–25 cm (8–10 in) in length, then plait three sausages together to make 6 small loaves.

4. Prove the loaves for 1 hour, until doubled in size. Brush the loaves with egg and scatter the sesame and poppy seeds over them.

5. Preheat the oven to 160°C (325°F) and bake for 17–20 minutes.

BASTARDS
DATE DE LIVRAISON: 25 DÉCEMBRE
PÈRE NOËL, AU PÔLE NORD

SERVICE POSTAL EXPRESS

CHALLAH **SANDWICHES**

MAKES **6** ✦ PREPARATION TIME: **1 HR** ✦ COOKING TIME: **17–20 MINS** ✦ RESTING TIME: **12 HRS + 1 HR 15 MINS**

EQUIPMENT
- Stand mixer, paddle
- Digital food thermometer
- Deep fryer

FOR 1 SANDWICH
- 300 g challah loaf
- 125 g crispy chicken
- 57 g omelette
- 32 g cabbage
- 44 g honey-mustard sauce

FOR THE CHALLAH DOUGH
- 596 g whole milk
- 165 g sunflower oil
- 870 g fine soft wheat flour (e.g., Italian 00 flour)
- 7 g salt
- 139 g caster (superfine) sugar
- 23 g fresh yeast

TO FINISH
- 1 egg, for glazing
- 10 g sesame seeds
- 10 g poppy seeds

FOR THE CRISPY CHICKEN
- 6 chicken breasts
- 120 g plain (all-purpose) flour
- 200 g eggs
- 350 g breadcrumbs
- Oil, for deep frying

FOR THE HONEY-MUSTARD SAUCE
- 96 g Dijon mustard
- 48 g wholegrain mustard
- 48 g honey
- 72 g sunflower oil

FOR THE CABBAGE
- 32 g cabbage

FOR THE OMELETTE
- 6 eggs
- a knob butter
- Salt and pepper

1. The day before, make the dough. Combine the milk and oil in the mixer fitted with the dough hook, followed by the dry ingredients. Add the yeast last. Run the mixer on low-medium speed. When the dough comes away from the sides of the bowl, stop the mixer and check the temperature, which should be 23–24°C (73–75°F). Transfer to a container and refrigerate overnight.

2. On the day, divide the dough into eighteen 100-g pieces and rest for 15 minutes. Shape each piece of dough into sausages 20–25 cm (8–10 in) in length, then plait three sausages together to make 6 small loaves.

3. Prove the loaves for 1 hour, until doubled in size. Brush the loaves with egg and scatter the sesame and poppy seeds over them.

4. Preheat the oven to 160 °C (325°F) and bake for 17–20 minutes.

5. Make the crispy chicken. Dip the breasts in the flour to coat, then in the beaten eggs and finally in the breadcrumbs. Pour oil into the deep fryer and heat to 140°C (284°F), then deep-fry the chicken until golden brown.

6. Make the sauce by mixing all the ingredients until smooth. Thinly slice the cabbage and mix with the sauce to make a coleslaw.

7. Make the omelette. Beat the eggs and season with salt and pepper. Melt the butter in a hot frying pan and add the beaten eggs (they should cover the entire surface of the pan). Cook the eggs until they are set enough to roll up the omelette. Transfer the rolled omelette to a chopping board and cut into 1 cm (½ in) wide slices.

8. Cut each challah loaf in half through the middle and fill with coleslaw, a piece of crispy chicken and omelette slices.

SAVOURY **BABKAS**

SERVES **6** ✦ PREPARATION TIME: **1 HR** ✦ COOKING TIME: **30 MINS** ✦ RESTING TIME: **24 HRS + 2 HRS 30 MINS**

EQUIPMENT
- **Stand mixer, dough hook**
- **Blender**
- **16 cm (6 in) stainless steel pastry ring**
- **Rolling pin**
- **Angled palette knife**
- **Pastry brush**
- **Baking parchment**

FOR THE BRIOCHE DOUGH
- **250g pastry (sponge) flour**
- **150g eggs**
- **5g salt**
- **53g caster (superfine) sugar**
- **10g whole milk**
- **8g fresh yeast**
- **125g unsalted butter**
- **1 egg, for glazing**

FOR THE PESTO
- **250g basil leaves**
- **50g Parmesan**
- **50g olive oil**
- **10g garlic**
- **15g pine nuts**
- **20g salt**
- **10g pepper**

FOR THE PESTO CREAM
- **400g mascarpone**

TO FINISH
- **102g tomato confit**
- **150g grated Emmental**

1. The day before, make the dough. In the mixer fitted with the dough hook, add the flour, eggs, salt, sugar, milk and yeast. Mix to form a dough and then knead. When the dough comes away from the sides of the bowl, incorporate the butter. When it comes away again, transfer the dough to container and refrigerate overnight.

2. On the day, make the pesto. Combine the ingredients in a blender and blend until smooth.

3. In a bowl, whisk the mascarpone with the pesto until smooth. Refrigerate until ready to use.

4. Take the dough out of the refrigerator and roll out to a rectangle with a thickness of 4 mm (⅛ in). Using the angled palette knife, spread the pesto cream over the entire surface. Add the tomato confit and grated cheese. Roll up the dough into a sausage and slice it into six equal portions. Arrange them in the pastry ring and allow to rise for 2 hours 30 minutes.

5. Preheat the oven to 160°C (325°F). Beat the egg and brush it over the top of the babka. Bake for 30 minutes.

6. Serve hot.

INVERTED **PUFF PASTRY**

SERVES **6** ✦ PREPARATION TIME: **40 MINS** ✦ RESTING TIME: **AT LEAST 12 HRS + 5 HRS**

EQUIPMENT
- **Stand mixer, dough hook, paddle**
- **Rolling pin**
- **Pastry brush**
- **Cling film (plastic wrap), guitar (acetate) sheet**

FOR THE DÉTREMPE
- **129g water**
- **8g white vinegar**
- **9g salt**
- **4g caster (superfine) sugar**
- **250g plain (all-purpose) flour**

FOR THE BEURRE MANIÉ
- **275g unsalted dry butter (84% fat)**
- **125g pastry (sponge) flour**

1. Leave the dry butter at room temperature for 12 hours before use.

2. Make the détrempe and beurre manié the day before you plan to make the puff pastry. To make the détrempe, combine the water, vinegar, salt, sugar and flour in the mixer fitted with the dough hook. Mix and then knead to a smooth dough. Gather the dough into a ball and place it on a wire rack lined with a guitar (acetate) sheet. Cover it with cling film (plastic wrap) and refrigerate for 12 hours.

3. Next, make the beurre manié. In the mixer fitted with the paddle, combine the softened dry butter with the flour and mix to a smooth paste that is easy to handle. Roll out the beurre manié to an even thickness. Refrigerate overnight.

4. On the day, roll out the détrempe to a width and length that will allow the beurre manié to be fully covered. Place the beurre manié in the middle of the détrempe and fold the sides over to encase the butter. Make three simple turns. Follow the step-by-step instructions and photographs on pages 152–153 as a guide, as the same technique for folding and turning dough is used.

5. Refrigerate for at least 5 hours.

6. Make another three simple turns.

Tip

You can make batches of puff pastry in advance and freeze them. Take them out and use them as needed.

THE FRENCH
BASTARDS

LATTICE

SERVES **6** ✦ PREPARATION TIME: **2 HRS** ✦ COOKING TIME: **1 HR 50 MINS** ✦ RESTING TIME: **36 HRS**

EQUIPMENT
- **Stand mixer, dough hook, paddle**
- **Lattice pastry cutter**
- **Rolling pin**
- **Pastry brush**
- **Cling film (plastic wrap), guitar (acetate) sheet**

FOR 1 PASTRY (TO SERVE 6)
- **900g inverted puff pastry**
- **600g roasted squash**
- **250g cooked spinach**
- **150g feta**

FOR THE DÉTREMPE
- **129g water**
- **8g white vinegar**
- **9g salt**
- **4g caster (superfine) sugar**
- **250g plain (all-purpose) flour**

FOR THE BEURRE MANIÉ
- **275g unsalted dry butter (84% fat)**
- **125g pastry (sponge) flour**

FOR THE HONEY-ROASTED SQUASH
- **500g winter squash**
- **60g honey**
- **20g olive oil**
- **3g flaked sea salt**
- **15g parsley**
- **2g pepper**

FOR THE SPINACH
- **20g olive oil**
- **200g baby spinach leaves**
- **20g unsalted butter**
- **10g water**

FOR THE GLAZE
- **1 egg**

1. Leave the dry butter at room temperature for 12 hours before use. Make the détrempe and beurre manié two days before you plan to make the pastry. To make the détrempe, combine the water, vinegar, salt, sugar and flour in the mixer fitted with the dough hook. Mix and then knead to a smooth dough. Gather the dough into a ball and place it on a wire rack lined with a guitar (acetate) sheet. Cover it with cling film (plastic wrap) and refrigerate for 12 hours.

2. Next, make the beurre manié. In the mixer fitted with the paddle, combine the softened dry butter with the flour and mix to a smooth paste that is easy to handle. Roll out the beurre manié to an even thickness. Refrigerate overnight.

3. The next day, roll out the détrempe to a width and length that will allow the beurre manié to be fully enclosed. Place the beurre manié in the middle of the détrempe and fold the sides over to encase the butter. Make three simple turns. Refrigerate for at least 5 hours, then make another three simple turns. Follow the step-by-step instructions and photographs on pages 152–153 as a guide, as the same technique for folding and turning dough is used.

4. Next, roast the squash. Cut open the squash and remove the seeds. Without peeling, coarsely cut it into pieces. Put the pieces into an ovenproof dish and add the honey, oil, salt, chopped parsley and pepper. Preheat the oven to 190°C (375°F). Roast for 50 minutes. The squash should be soft and golden brown.

5. Cook the spinach. Heat the oil in a pan and add the spinach. When the leaves start to wilt, add the butter. Let it melt, then deglaze with the water.

6. Roll out the puff pastry to a thickness of 2 mm (1⁄16 in). Have ready a pastry brush and a little water. Cut out two 25 × 9 cm (10 × 3½ in) rectangles. Leaving a 1.5 cm (½ in) margin around the edges, cover the first rectangle with the spinach, followed by the honey-roasted squash and finally the feta. Run the lattice cutter vertically over the second pastry rectangle, then pull the edges a little apart to create a lattice effect. Brush the uncovered edge of the topped pastry with water, place the lattice over the filling and seal the edges well. Refrigerate overnight.

7. On the day, preheat the oven to 170°C (340°F). Brush the pastry with beaten egg and bake for 1 hour.

BOUREKAS

MAKES **6** ✦ PREPARATION TIME: **2 HRS** ✦ COOKING TIME: **30 MINS** ✦ RESTING TIME: **36 HRS**

EQUIPMENT
- **Stand mixer, dough hook, paddle**
- **Rolling pin**
- **Piping bag**
- **Pastry brush**
- **Cling film (plastic wrap), guitar (acetate) sheet**

FOR 1 BOUREKA
- **150g inverted puff pastry**
- **100 g feta béchamel sauce**

FOR THE DÉTREMPE
- **129g water**
- **8g white vinegar**
- **9g salt**
- **4g caster (superfine) sugar**
- **250g plain (all-purpose) flour**

FOR THE BEURRE MANIÉ
- **125g pastry (sponge) flour**
- **275g unsalted dry butter (84% fat)**

FOR THE FETA BÉCHAMEL SAUCE
- **100g unsalted butter**
- **100g plain (all-purpose) flour**
- **200g whole milk**
- **10g salt**
- **10g pepper**
- **180g feta**

TO FINISH
- **1 egg, for glazing**
- **20 g sesame seeds**

1. Leave the dry butter at room temperature for 12 hours before use.

2. Make the détrempe and beurre manié two days before you plan to make the pastry. To make the détrempe, combine the water, vinegar, salt, sugar and flour in the mixer fitted with the dough hook. Mix and then knead to a smooth dough. Gather the dough into a ball and place it on a wire rack lined with a guitar (acetate) sheet. Cover it with cling film (plastic wrap) and refrigerate for 12 hours.

3. Next, make the beurre manié. In the mixer fitted with the paddle, combine the softened dry butter with the flour and mix to a smooth paste that is easy to handle. Roll out the beurre manié to an even thickness. Refrigerate overnight.

4. The next day, roll out the détrempe to a width and length that will allow the beurre manié to be fully enclosed. Place the beurre manié in the middle of the détrempe and fold the sides over to encase the butter. Make three simple turns. Refrigerate for at least 5 hours, then make another three simple turns. Follow the step-by-step instructions and photographs on pages 152–153 as a guide.

5. Make the béchamel sauce. Melt the butter in a saucepan, then remove from the heat and incorporate the flour to form a roux. Return the pan to a low heat and allow the mixture to dry out a little, then add the milk. Stir constantly to the desired consistency. Season with salt and pepper and stir in the crumbled feta until well incorporated. Allow the béchamel sauce to cool, then transfer to a piping bag and refrigerate.

6. Roll out the puff pastry to a thickness of 2 mm (1⁄16 in). Prepare a brush and a little water. Cut out six 12 cm (5 in) squares from the pastry. Pipe béchamel sauce over the top of the squares, then fold them into triangles with the sauce inside. Refrigerate overnight.

7. On the day, preheat the oven to 170°C (340°F). Brush the beaten egg over the pastries and scatter over the sesame seeds. Using the tip of a knife, cut small holes into the pastries and bake for 30 minutes.

Tip
Drizzle a little honey over the bourekas before serving.

SANDWICH **BREAD**

SERVES **6** ✦ PREPARATION TIME: **20 MINS** ✦ COOKING TIME: **30 MINS** ✦ RESTING TIME: **1 HR 40 MINS**

EQUIPMENT
- **Stand mixer, dough hook**
- **Rolling pin**
- **Loaf tin (pan)**

FOR THE BREAD DOUGH
- **80g water**
- **80g whole milk**
- **50g egg**
- **4g salt**
- **250g plain (all-purpose) flour**
- **25g caster (superfine) sugar**
- **3g fresh yeast**
- **15g unsalted butter**

TO GLAZE
- **1 egg**

1. In the mixer fitted with the dough hook, combine the water, milk and egg. Add the salt, flour, sugar and yeast (add the yeast last because it must not be in contact with the salt). Mix for 4 minutes on the lowest speed to form a dough.

2. Add the butter, cut into pieces. Increase the speed to high and knead for 6 minutes. The butter should be perfectly incorporated and the dough smooth.

3. When the dough comes away from the sides of the bowl, transfer it to a greased bowl, cover it with a cloth and rest for 45 minutes at room temperature.

4. Transfer the dough to a greased or floured work surface and divide into two 250 g pieces. Cover with a cloth and leave to rise for 10 minutes.

5. Using the rolling pin, deflate each piece of dough while rolling it out into a rectangle, then roll up each rectangle into a sausage. Grease the loaf tin (pan) and place the two sausages lengthways side by side inside. Cover with a cloth and prove for 45 minutes at room temperature.

6. Preheat the oven to 180°C (350°F). The dough should have risen to the top of the tin. Brush the top of the dough with beaten egg and bake for 25 minutes.

7. Turn the loaf out of the tin and return it to the oven to bake for a further 5 minutes. Allow to cool on a wire rack.

THE FRENCH
BASTARDS

BASTARD **SANDOS**

MAKES **6** ✦ PREPARATION TIME: **1 HR 30 MINS** ✦ COOKING TIME: **1 HR** ✦ RESTING TIME: **1 HR 40 MINS**

EQUIPMENT
- Stand mixer, dough hook
- Loaf tin (pan)

FOR 1 BASTARD SANDO
- 83g sandwich bread
- 108g caramelised onions
- 116g pastrami
- 44g honey-mustard sauce

FOR THE BREAD DOUGH
- 250g plain (all-purpose) flour
- 25g caster (superfine) sugar
- 4g salt
- 80g whole milk
- 3g fresh yeast
- 80g water
- 50g egg
- 15g unsalted butter
- 1 egg, for glazing

FOR THE CARAMELISED ONIONS
- 500g white onions
- 50g unsalted butter
- 50g sugar
- 50g water

FOR THE PASTRAMI
- 700g pastrami

FOR THE HONEY-MUSTARD SAUCE
- 96g Dijon mustard
- 48g wholegrain mustard
- 48g honey
- 72g sunflower oil

1. Make the bread. In the mixer fitted with the dough hook, combine the water, milk and eggs. Add the salt, flour, sugar and yeast (add the yeast last because it must not be in contact with the salt). Mix for 4 minutes on the lowest speed to form a dough. Add the butter, cut into pieces, increase the speed to high and knead for 6 minutes. The butter should be perfectly incorporated and the dough smooth. When the dough comes away from the sides of the bowl, transfer it to a greased bowl, cover it with a cloth and rest for 45 minutes at room temperature.

2. Transfer the dough to a greased or floured work surface and divide into two 250 g pieces. Cover with a cloth and leave to rise for 10 minutes.

3. Using the rolling pin, deflate each piece of dough while rolling it out into a rectangle. Roll up each rectangle into a sausage. Grease the loaf tin (pan) and place the two sausages lengthways side by side inside. Cover with a cloth and prove for 45 minutes at room temperature.

4. Meanwhile, make the caramelised onions. Peel and thinly slice the onions. Melt the butter in a saucepan and sauté the onions for a few minutes, then add the sugar. Allow the onions to caramelise over a low heat for 30 minutes, stirring constantly. When the onions start to darken, add the water a little at a time.

5. Preheat the oven to 180°C (375°F). The dough should have risen to the top of the tin. Brush the top of the dough with beaten egg and bake for 25 minutes.

6. Turn the loaf out of the tin and return it to the oven to bake for a further 5 minutes. Allow to cool on a wire rack.

7. Make the sauce by mixing all the ingredients until smooth.

8. Very thinly slice the pastrami.

9. Cut the loaf into 2 cm (¾ in) thick slices and lay them out the work surface. Put a heaped tablespoon of caramelised onions on the slices that will serve as the base and add a little sauce. Top with a few slices of pastrami and cover with the top slices to make sandwiches.

HOT
Coffee
Berghain 07 | Part II
BAKED
BASTARDS

CHARCOAL-SESAME **BAGUETTE**

SERVES **6** ✦ PREPARATION TIME: **1 HR 30 MINS** ✦ COOKING TIME: **25 MINS + 1 HR**
RESTING TIME: **2 HRS 30 MINS + 24 HRS + 1 HR 15 MINS**

EQUIPMENT
- **Stand mixer, dough hook**
- **Baking tray (pan)**

FOR THE BREAD DOUGH
- **279 g strong white flour**
- **22 g sourdough starter**
- **5 g salt**
- **1 g fresh yeast**
- **196 g water**

FOR THE SESAME MIXTURE
- **56 g sesame seeds**
- **31 g cold water**
- **11 g food-grade activated charcoal**

1. The day before, make the sesame mixture. Preheat the oven to 180°C (375°F). Spread the sesame seeds out on a baking tray (pan) and toast them in the oven for 25 minutes. Mix them immediately with the cold water and add the charcoal.

2. Next, combine all the ingredients for the dough in the mixer fitted with the dough hook, then rest for 1 hour. Run the mixer on the lowest speed for 4 minutes to form a dough. Knead the dough on the same speed for 10 minutes, then set to low-medium speed and knead for 1–2 minutes. Incorporate the sesame mixture and knead on low speed for a further 5 minutes, then on speed 2 for 1 minute. Rest the dough for 30 minutes, then knead on low speed for 5 seconds. Cover the mixer bowl with a damp cloth and rest the dough for 45–60 minutes, then refrigerate for 24 hours.

3. On the day, roll the dough into a ball on a floured work surface and allow it to rest for 15 minutes. Shape the baguette as desired and leave it to rise for 1 hour.

4. Place a baking tray (pan) inside the oven and preheat to 240°C (475°F) with a pan of water on the bottom shelf. Using a sharp knife, score the baguette. Transfer the baguette to the hot baking tray and bake for 15 minutes. Lower the temperature to 200°C (400°F) and bake for a further 45 minutes.

5. Remove from the oven and allow to cool, preferably on a wire rack.

SALMON & CHARCOAL-SESAME **SANDWICHES**

MAKES **6** ✦ PREPARATION TIME: **3 HRS** ✦ COOKING TIME: **25 MINS + 1 HR**
RESTING TIME: **2 HRS 30 MINS + 24 HRS + 1 HR 15 MINS**

EQUIPMENT
- **Stand mixer, dough hook**
- **Baking tray (pan)**
- **Baking parchment**

FOR 1 SANDWICH
- **2 slices charcoal sesame baguette**
- **96g herb cream cheese**
- **100g gravlax (cured salmon)**
- **3 tomatoes**
- **15g rocket (arugula)**
- **Olive oil**
- **Salt and pepper**

FOR THE BREAD
- **279g strong white flour**
- **22g sourdough starter**
- **5g salt**
- **1g fresh yeast**
- **196g water**

FOR THE SESAME MIXTURE
- **56g sesame seeds**
- **31g water**
- **11g food-grade activated charcoal**

FOR THE HERB CREAM CHEESE
- **70g Philadelphia® cream cheese**
- **15g chives**
- **11g lemon juice**

1. Bake the bread at least 24 hours before making the sandwich. Start by making the sesame mixture. Preheat the oven to 180°C (375°F). Spread the sesame seeds out on a baking tray (pan) and toast them in the oven for 25 minutes. Mix them immediately with the cold water and add the charcoal.

2. Next, combine all the ingredients for the dough in the mixer fitted with the dough hook, then rest for 1 hour. Run the mixer on the lowest speed for 4 minutes to form a dough. Knead the dough on the same speed for 10 minutes, then set to low-medium speed and knead for 1–2 minutes. Incorporate the sesame mixture and knead on low speed for a further 5 minutes, then on speed 2 for 1 minute. Rest the dough for 30 minutes and then knead on low for 5 seconds. Cover the mixer bowl with a damp cloth and rest the dough for 45–60 minutes, then refrigerate for 24 hours.

3. On the day, roll the dough into a ball on a floured work surface and leave it to rest for 15 minutes. Shape the baguette as desired and allow it to rise for 1 hour.

4. Place a baking tray (pan) inside the oven and preheat to 240°C (475°F) with a pan of water on the bottom shelf. Using a sharp knife, score the baguette. Transfer the baguette to the hot baking tray and bake for 15 minutes. Lower the temperature to 200°C (400°F) and bake for a further 45 minutes.

5. Remove from the oven and allow to cool, preferably on a wire rack, then cut the baguette into 2 cm (¾ in) thick slices.

6. Wash and very thinly slice the tomatoes. Very thinly slice the salmon. Season the rocket with oil, salt and pepper.

7. Spread all the bread slices with the cream cheese. Make a good layer of tomato slices on half of them. Cover with the salmon slices and rocket and top with the remaining bread. Wrap the sandwiches in baking parchment and cut them in half.

TRADITIONAL **PAVÉ LOAF**

SERVES **6** ✦ PREPARATION TIME: **40 MINS** ✦ COOKING TIME: **1 HR** ✦ RESTING TIME: **2 HRS + 24 HRS**

EQUIPMENT
- **Stand mixer, dough hook**
- **Baking tray (pan)**

FOR THE BREAD DOUGH
- **167g strong white flour**
- **117g water**
- **13g sourdough starter**
- **3g salt**
- **1g fresh yeast**

1. Make this loaf 24 hours before use. Combine all the ingredients for the dough in the mixer fitted with the dough hook, then rest for 1 hour. Run the mixer on the lowest speed for 4 minutes to form a dough. Knead the dough on the same speed for 10 minutes, then set to low-medium and knead for 1–2 minutes. Knead on low speed for a further 5 seconds.

2. Cover the mixer bowl with a damp cloth and rest the dough for 45–60 minutes, then refrigerate for 24 hours.

3. On the day, place a baking tray (pan) inside the oven and preheat to 240°C (475°F) with a pan of water on the bottom shelf. Transfer the dough to a work surface and score the top with a sharp knife. Place the loaf on the hot baking tray and bake for 15 minutes. Lower the temperature to 200°C (400°F) and bake for a further 45 minutes.

4. Remove from the oven and allow to cool, preferably on a wire rack.

BÂTARDE **LOAF**

SERVES **6** ✦ PREPARATION TIME: **40 MINS** ✦ COOKING TIME: **1 HR** ✦ RESTING TIME: **2 HRS 30 MINS + 24 HRS + 1 HR 30 MINS**

EQUIPMENT
- **Stand mixer, dough hook**
- **Baking tray (pan)**

FOR THE BREAD DOUGH
- **117 g strong white flour**
- **37 g wholemeal flour**
- **13 g rye flour**
- **13 g stiff sourdough starter**
- **3 g salt**
- **1 g fresh yeast**
- **240 g water**

1. Make the dough 24 hours before use. Combine all the ingredients for the dough in the mixer fitted with the dough hook, then rest for 1 hour. Run the mixer on the lowest speed for 4 minutes to form a dough. Knead the dough on the same speed for 10 minutes, then set to low-medium speed and knead for 1–2 minutes.

2. Rest the dough for 30 minutes in the mixer bowl at room temperature. Knead on low speed for a further 5 seconds.

3. Cover the mixer bowl with a damp cloth and rest the dough for 45 minutes–1 hour, then refrigerate for 24 hours.

4. On the day, roll the dough into a ball on a floured work surface and allow it to rest for 15 minutes. Shape the loaf as desired and leave to rise for 1 hour.

5. Place a baking tray (pan) inside the oven and preheat to 240°C (475°F) with a pan of water on the bottom shelf. On the work surface, score the top of the loaf with a sharp knife. Place the loaf on the hot baking tray and bake for 15 minutes. Lower the temperature to 200°C (400°F) and bake for a further 45 minutes.

6. Remove from the oven and allow to cool, preferably on a wire rack.

THE FRE
BASTAR
AISON FONDÉE

RYE **LOAF**

SERVES **6** ✦ PREPARATION TIME: **30 MINS** ✦ COOKING TIME : **1 HR 20 MINS** ✦ RESTING TIME: **2 HRS 30 MINS**

EQUIPMENT
- **Stand mixer, dough hook**
- **Round banneton (proofing basket)**

FOR THE BREAD DOUGH
- **220g rye flour**
- **198g stiff sourdough starter**
- **4g salt**
- **209g water**

1. Combine the flour, sourdough starter and salt in the mixer fitted with the dough hook.

2. In a saucepan, heat the water to 82°C (180°F).

3. Add it to the mixer and run the mixer on low-medium speed for 4 minutes.

4. Rest the dough for 1 hour 30 minutes at room temperature.

5. Transfer the dough to a well-floured work surface, shape into a ball and place in a floured banneton. Cover with a cloth and prove for 1 hour.

6. Preheat the oven to 240°C (475°F) and place a pan of water on the bottom shelf. Bake for 15 minutes, then lower the temperature to 200°C (400°F) and bake for a further 50 minutes.

7. Turn the loaf out of the tin and return it to the oven for a further 15 minutes at the same temperature.

8. Remove from the oven and allow to cool, preferably on a wire rack.

FRENCH
DATE DE
PÈRE

BAGELS

SERVES **6** ✦ PREPARATION TIME: **40 MINS** ✦ COOKING TIME: **15–17 MINS** ✦ RESTING TIME: **2 HRS**

EQUIPMENT
- **Stand mixer, dough hook**
- **Baking tray (pan)**
- **Baking parchment**
- **Pastry brush**

FOR THE BREAD DOUGH
- **208 g fine soft wheat flour (e.g., Italian 00 flour)**
- **8 g caster (superfine) sugar**
- **4 g salt**
- **2 g fresh yeast**
- **102 g cold water**
- **11 g sunflower oil**
- **6 g honey**

FOR THE POACHING LIQUID
- **1,201 kg water**
- **2 g bicarbonate of soda (baking soda)**

TO FINISH
- **1 egg, for glazing**
- **Seeds of your choice: black and white sesame seeds, poppy seeds, etc.**

1. Make the dough. Combine all the ingredients in the mixer fitted with the dough hook. Run the mixer on the lowest speed for 6 minutes and then on low-medium speed for 10–15 minutes to form a smooth dough.

2. Transfer the dough to a well-oiled dish and rest for 30 minutes at room temperature.

3. Divide the dough into two portions, each weighing 170 g, then roll them into three balls each.

4. Rest the dough for 30 minutes at room temperature.

5. Using a knife, cut a hole in the middle of each dough portion and then enlarge it to give the pieces a bagel shape.

6. Prove the bagels for 1 hour on a baking tray (pan) lined with baking parchment.

7. In a saucepan, bring the water and bicarbonate of soda for the poaching liquid to the boil and then carefully add the bagels. Poach for 30 seconds on each side.

8. Transfer the bagels to a sheet of baking parchment, brush with the egg and scatter over the seeds.

9. Preheat the oven to 240°C (475°F), then bake the bagels for 15–20 minutes.

BATARDE
AUX GRAINES
1,50€
TRADITION
1,20€
THE FRENCH
PAIN AUX
NOIX
14,80€/KG
PAIN AU
SARRASIN
9,80€/KG
TOURTE
DE SEIGLE
9,60€/KG
TOURTE
PETIT EPEAUTRE
INTEGRAL
12,80€/KG

Exécutif Chef

HERB & OLIVE **CIABATTA ROLLS**

MAKES **6** ✦ PREPARATION TIME: **40 MINS** ✦ COOKING TIME: **15–20 MINS** ✦ RESTING TIME: **2 HRS + 12 HRS + 30–45 MINS**

EQUIPMENT
- **Stand mixer, dough hook**
- **Baking tray (pan)**
- **Baking parchment**

FOR THE FILLING
- **60g black olives, stoned (pitted) and halved**
- **5g herbes de Provence**
- **Olive oil**

FOR THE BREAD DOUGH
- **167g strong white flour**
- **50g liquid sourdough starter**
- **4g salt**
- **1g fresh yeast**
- **100g cold water**
- **60g olive oil**

1. Mix the halved olives with the herbs and oil.

2. Make the dough. Combine all the ingredients, except the oil, in the mixer fitted with the dough hook. Run the mixer on the lowest speed for 6 minutes, then set to speed 2 and knead for 6 minutes. Set the mixer to speed 1 and add the olive oil in a thin stream until fully incorporated, then set the mixer to speed 2 and knead for 5 minutes. Reduce the speed again and add the herb and olive mixture.

3. Transfer the dough to a well-oiled dish and rest for 2 hours at room temperature.

4. On a floured work surface, knead the dough by hand to deflate.

5. Rest the deflated dough in the refrigerator for at least 12 hours.

6. Return the dough to a floured work surface and, without deflating, cut it into six uniform rectangles and place them on a baking tray (pan) lined with baking parchment.

7. Prove at room temperature for 30–45 minutes.

8. Preheat the oven to 240°C (475°F) and place a pan of water inside, then bake the rolls for 15–20 minutes.

9. Remove from the oven and brush the top of each ciabatta roll with olive oil.

SOURDOUGH **FOUGASSE**

SERVES **6** ✦ PREPARATION TIME: **40 MINS** ✦ COOKING TIME: **10–15 MINS** ✦ RESTING TIME: **30 MINS + 12 HRS + 1 HR 15 MINS**

EQUIPMENT
- **Stand mixer, dough hook**
- **Rolling pin**
- **Baking tray (pan)**
- **Baking parchment**

FOR 1 FOUGASSE
- **60g white onion**
- **3g curry powder**
- **Parmesan**
- **Olive oil**

FOR THE BREAD DOUGH
- **167g strong white flour**
- **33g liquid sourdough starter**
- **3g salt**
- **1g fresh yeast**
- **113g cold water**
- **15g olive oil**

1. Peel and chop the onion and mix with the curry powder.

2. Make the dough. Combine all the ingredients, except the oil, in the mixer fitted with the dough hook. Run the mixer on the lowest speed for 4 minutes, then set to low-medium and knead for 4 minutes. Set the mixer to low and add the olive oil in a thin stream until fully incorporated, then set the mixer to low-medium and knead for 5 minutes. Reduce the speed again and add the onion mixture.

3. Transfer the dough to a well-oiled dish and rest for 30 minutes at room temperature.

4. On a floured work surface, knead the dough by hand to deflate.

5. Rest the deflated dough in the refrigerator for at least 12 hours.

6. Return the dough to a floured work surface and, without deflating, roll it into a ball.

7. Rest the dough in the refrigerator for 15 minutes, then roll it out with a rolling pin into a flat oval shape. Transfer to a baking tray (pan) lined with baking parchment.

8. Prove for 1 hour at room temperature.

9. Make five diagonal cuts on each side of the dough in a leaf design and stretch them open to keep them from closing when baked.

10. Scatter over Parmesan shavings or grated Parmesan.

11. Preheat the oven to 240°C (400°F) and place a pan of water inside, then bake the fougasse for 10–15 minutes.

12. Remove from the oven and brush the top with olive oil.

BRIOCHE **LOAF**

SERVES **6** ✦ PREPARATION TIME: **30 MINS** ✦ COOKING TIME: **15–18 MINS** ✦ RESTING TIME: **12 HRS + 2 HRS**

EQUIPMENT
- **Stand mixer, dough hook**
- **Rolling pin**
- **Loaf tin (pan)**

FOR THE BRIOCHE DOUGH
- **250g pastry (sponge) flour**
- **150g eggs**
- **5g salt**
- **53g caster (superfine) sugar**
- **10g whole milk**
- **8g fresh yeast**
- **125g unsalted butter**

1. The day before, make the dough. In the mixer fitted with the dough hook, add the flour, eggs, salt, sugar, milk and yeast. Mix to form a dough and then knead. When the dough comes away from the sides of the bowl, incorporate the butter. When it comes away again, transfer it to container and refrigerate overnight.

2. On the day, take the dough out of the refrigerator 20–30 minutes before use. Roll out the dough to a thickness of 3 mm (⅛ in), then roll it up into a sausage and cut it in half lengthways. Grease the loaf tin (pan) and place the two sausages lengthways side by side inside. Cover with a cloth and prove for 2 hours.

3. Preheat the oven to 160°C (325°F) and bake for 15–18 minutes.

GLOSSARY

BAIN-MARIE
A hot water bath used for gently cooking.

BREAD IMPROVER
Helps to make dough easier to shape and less likely to shrink, contributing to a lighter, airier bread with a desirable crumb.

CASE
Pastry base that is filled to make certain pastries.

COCOA NIBS
Small pieces of cacao bean that remain after the outer husk has been removed. They have a rich, intense chocolate flavour.

COMPOUND CHOCOLATE
Chocolate that uses vegetable fat, such as coconut oil, in place of cocoa butter.

CONICAL SIEVE
A utensil used to filter stocks and other liquids with holes of variable size.

COUVERTURE CHOCOLATE
Chocolate used for moulding, dipping, and coating, it has a high cocoa butter content, which results in a glossy finish.

DEFLATE
To remove the gas formed when dough is left to rise or to stop it from rising.

DEGERM
Remove the germ from a garlic clove.

DÉTREMPE
A dough made from flour, water and salt that is used to make puff pastry.

DILUTE
To give a preparation or mixture, such as a batter, a more fluid consistency by adding a liquid component.

DOUGH FORMATION
• When flour, water and other ingredients are mixed and start to form a solid substance.
• The start of the pastry and bread-making process.

DRY BUTTER
Butter with a high fat content used to make puff pastry.

FINISH A SAUCE (WITH BUTTER)
To incorporate small pieces of butter into a sauce by rotating the container or by using a spoon or whisk.

GLAZE
• To make a preparation glossy at the end of the cooking process by dusting with icing sugar or syrup and placing in the oven to caramelise the sugar (e.g. apple fritters).
• To brush beaten egg or egg yolk over pastry or dough to give it a glossy finish.

GUITAR (ACETATE) SHEET
A guitar sheet is made of plastic (smooth or patterned) and is used to give chocolate a glossy finish.

ICE
To cover a cake or pastry with icing (frosting) or chocolate coating.

INVERTED PUFF PASTRY
Inverted puff pastry differs from traditional puff pastry in that the beurre manié, made with a larger amount of flour, is used to encase the détrempe, producing fluffier layers.

INVERTED SUGAR
Liquid syrup made from sugar and water. Also known as invert sugar and invert sugar syrup.

KNEAD
To press or work a dough to make it smooth.

LINE
To cover the bottom and sides of a tart mould or pastry ring with pastry (puff pastry, shortcrust pastry, sweet pastry, etc.).

MIXTURE
A combination of several ingredients used to make a dish or dessert.

NAMELAKA
A Japanese term meaning 'ultra creamy'. Similar to ganache but more delicate and airier.

PASTRY (SPONGE) FLOUR
Flour with a finer texture and lower protein content than plain (all-purpose) flour.

PECTIN NH
A gelling agent often used for glazes and fillings.

PIPING BAG
A nylon piping bag with a nozzle (plain or patterned) is more watertight and easier to maintain than the old fabric ones. This piping bag makes it easier to give shape to a batter or other semi-solid mixtures formed on a baking tray (pan) or to decorate a pastry. Piping bags are now available in disposable plastic. Piping syringes are also becoming popular.

PIPING NOZZLE
A metal or plastic cone used at the end of a plastic or cloth piping bag for decorating; it comes in different shapes and sizes.

PUFF PASTRY
Puff pastry is a pastry comprising different layers made by alternating dough with butter.

RELAX
To soften a dough by kneading it for a long time, making it stretchier.

ROLL OUT
To flatten dough with a rolling pin to the desired thickness.

ROUX
A simple mixture of butter and flour in equal proportions that is cooked for varying lengths of time.

SAND
To knead butter with flour or other ingredients such as sugar without the addition of liquid until it resembles very fine crumbs that look like sand.

SCATTER OVER
To gradually add a powdered ingredient, including baking powder, flour, etc.

SIFT
To separate any lumps out of flour or icing (powdered) sugar with a sieve.

SOAK
To brush or drizzle a liqueur, alcohol or syrup over a cake to flavour it and make it moist.

SOFTENED BUTTER
Butter left out or worked to a spreadable consistency.

SOFT PEAKS
When egg whites are beaten to a consistency where they curl downwards on the whisk, like a bird's beak.

VERGOISE BLONDE SUGAR
A soft, light-coloured brown sugar, with a subtle caramel flavour, that is produced from sugar beet. It has a moist texture, making it ideal for use in pastries and desserts.

WHITE VINEGAR
A clear, colourless vinegar typically containing 4–7% acetic acid.

INDEX

Quadrille, Penguin Random House UK,
One Embassy Gardens,
8 Viaduct Gardens, London SW11 7BW

Quadrille Publishing Limited is part of the Penguin Random House group of companies whose addresses can be found at global.penguinrandomhouse.com

First published in 2022 by Hachette Cuisine with the French title *Boulangerie, Pâtisserie, Bastarderie*. Published in the English language by agreement with Hachette Pratique.

Published by Quadrille in 2025

www.penguin.co.uk

A CIP catalogue record for this book is available from the British Library.

ISBN 978 1 83783 485 3

10 9 8 7 6 5 4 3 2 1

Managing Director, Publishing: Sarah Lavelle
Publishing Director: Kajal Mistry
Senior Commissioning Editor: Eve Marleau
Copy Editor: Judith Hannam
Proofreader: Joe Shakespeare
Cover design: Stuart Hardie
Internal design: Zero Zoro
Photographer: Géraldine Martens
Production Director: Stephen Lang
Production Manager: Sabeena Atchia

Colour reproduction by p2d

Printed in China by C&C Offset Printing Co., Ltd.

The authorised representative in the EEA is Penguin Random House Ireland, Morrison Chambers, 32 Nassau Street, Dublin D02 YH68.

Penguin Random House is committed to a sustainable future for our business, our readers and our planet. This book is made from Forest Stewardship Council® certified paper.